OUTSIDE THE CAVE

2

GEORGIA S. McDADE

Outside the Cave 2 © 2015, 2019 Georgia S. McDade

All rights reserved. No part of this publication may be reproduced or transmitted in any form or by any means, electronic or mechanical, including photocopy, recording, or any information storage and retrieval system now known or to be invented, without permission in writing of the author, except by reviewers who wish to quote brief passages in connection with a review written for publication in print and electronic form.

Cover Art © Adam Korpak

Book & Cover Design by Vladimir Verano, Vertvolta design
www.vertvoltapress.com

Contact the author:

gsmcdade@msn.com

SECOND EDITION

ISBN: 978-0-9821872-0-3

Always hoping a word, a sentence, gesture, or act will help someone, I dedicate *Outside the Cave II* to all of the people who want all of the people unconditionally all of the time and everywhere to be treated as the human beings they are.

ACKNOWLEDGEMENTS

Thanks go to the persons who granted me permission to use their art in *Outside the Cave II*:
Thomas Ager
Jessica Dodge
Susan Gans
Jessaca Madlock
Scott Mansfield
Selma Waldman
Adam Korpak for his illustrations and the cover.

Thanks to Iris M. Hodge for suggestions and editing.

I am especially grateful to all of the persons who read my works and took the time to tell me what they see in the works. It was the encouragement of these readers that prompted me to collect and write poetry for this volume.

Thank you.

CONTENTS

(Poems listed in the order they appear in the book.)

FROM THE AUTHOR	i
ALL IFS AND THENS	1
RELIEVING PRESSURE	2
FREEDOM—OR THE LACK THEREOF	3
SUGGESTIONS	4
HOW MUCH?	5
MEMORY, WHAT WE REMEMBER	6
REASSESSMENT	7
A STANDSTILL	8
OBSCENITY	10
TWINS BORN AT DIFFERENT TIMES	11
OBSTACLES	13
A BIO	14
ESCAPISTS	15
THERE IS NO HALF-TIME	16
WHAT SHE HAS BECOME	17
FROM LIKE TO DISLIKE	19
NO BOOTS ON THE GROUND	20
AN ATTEMPT AT HUMOR	21
THE HAND AND TIME	24
VOWS BROKEN	25
MUSINGS	27
THE HELP	29
EXCUSES	29
THE QUICK AND THE DEAD	30
LIMITS	30
FAMILIARITY	31

Mind and Matter	32
Words	32
Windmills—Or Not	33
Letting Someone In	34
Observation	35
Being Slow	36
Not Enough Time	37
Flags	38
Few Corrections	39
Choices	40
The Photographer Artist	41
Chaos	42
Not Always Possible	43
My Head Tapes	44
Things to Do	45
Why?	46
The Subjectivity of Objectivity	48
The Paradox of Handling	49
It's a Wrap	50
I Ask Why	51
A Patch of Ground	52
Molehills Becoming Mountains	53
Brainprint	54
Beliefs	56
Special Songs	57
The Nastiest Word	59
Maggots	61
Innocent Eggs	62

I Wish…	63
Terror Colors	64
Georgia's Law	65
Moving On	66
Matt	67
Opportunities	69
Lies	70
The Lie Continues	71
Religion and Guns	73
Art Interrupts	74
Selected Stories	76
Mama Nadi Confesses	77
Promise Kept	78
Soaring	79
Routine	80
Real Mistakes	81
Dependent Clauses	81
Frogs and Princes	82
The Problem with Memories	83
The Little Nothing Dress	85
If You Lived Here…	87
Attention!	88
Michael	89
Sleep	90
Age	91
Georgia's Time	93
Make the Call	94
To the Folks Who Did Not Want the Divorce*	95

Evidence	98
Tests	99
Figs, Pomegranates, and Grapes	100
What If?	101
The Inconvenience of Being Intelligent	103
Detour	105
Galloping	107
Makings	108
Desperation	109
Misreading	110
The Other Brother: The Non-Prodigal Son	111
No Ram in the Bushes	112
No Compromise	114
Ways	115
Michelangelo Unfinished	116
Journeys	117
The Right Thing	118
The Impossible Win	119
The Straw Speaks	120
Visitors	121
Hair Hazards	123
Elephant in the Room	124
My Poems	125
Why I Won't Let It Go	126
Passing Moments	128
Crazy Men	129
Observing the Creative Process	130
The Way Some of Us Are	132

CREATED TO DO GOD'S WORK	133
SLIP-SLIDING SYNDROME	137
HUGS AND WORDS	138
UNDER THE BIG TOP I	139
UNDER THE BIG TOP II	141
A DOZEN COMMANDMENTS TO KNOW	143
WHEN DID IT BEGIN?	144
WARFARE	146
VOCABULARY BUILDING	147
THE FRAY	148
RELATIONSHIPS	149
THE CHANGE	150
DEAD SOLDIERS	151
TWO WOMEN TALK ABOUT DEATH, BRIEFLY	152
DEMANDS	153
THIRTY TIME	154
CHARACTERS	156
INDEX	161
ABOUT THE AUTHOR	167

From the Author

One wants a Teller in a time like this. ~ Gwendolyn Brooks

A STORYWRITER BY NATURE, I decided to participate in writers' group in 1991. As most of my fellow writers wrote poems, I continued to write stories. I was content to have a poem or two in an anthology, but I saw myself as a storywriter who had written a few poems.

One day, in preparing for a public reading in which each member of the group was allotted only ten minutes, I elected not to participate because my story required twenty-one minutes. The group, however, voted to allow me twenty-one minutes through creative timesharing. Grateful though I was, I felt guilty having to use twice the amount of time as other members. Since I enjoyed the support and feedback of the group, I resolved to attempt to express my thoughts within the context of poetical compositions, at least for readings. Initially I struggled to convey my feelings and ideas with fewer words. But with patience and practice, I was surprised how often the format of a poem allowed me to express perceptions and ideas fully and exactly.

Another breakthrough event was being invited to write poems based on my reflections on the art in a gallery in Seattle's Pioneer Square. Each month, for almost four years, I wrote poems inspired by the work of at least two artists in a variety of media. The silent yet vocal presentations of the visual art compelled me to write more poems. Very often I put to paper thoughts and experiences that had been in my head for years or ideas I felt intuitively but had never expressed. These and other poetic expressions have resonated, in some way, with diverse audiences who wanted to share them with other friends.

I had my first book of poems, *Outside the Cave*, published in 2009, and I was pleased with the product as well as the reception my work received from friends and strangers.

My poetry examines many subjects and issues, but a common theme I observe is the unique human experience of everyday living. Sometimes by exposing the humor and the tragedy of encounters, missed opportunities, diminished dreams, I come away with a deeper awareness of our existence. I share what I see and feel in a way that I hope contributes to better understanding of self and others. I want others to see and understand MORE, not necessarily agree or disagree, but see: people, loss, inequality, time, war, the world in a way that brings openness rather than restriction. Too often is there tension caused by the difference of ideas between two persons or groups. Too often words and attitudes are presented as the only way possible. Awareness is an evolution that opens us to ourselves and others. Weighing, judging, deciding, selecting takes time and may create tension. Usually my discoveries help me avoid paralysis by alleviating or ending the tension writing.

This expressed awareness I hope you enjoy as my poetry may do the same for you.

Georgia S. McDade, Ph. D. March 2012

OUTSIDE THE CAVE II

All Ifs and Thens

If there had been candy in the house, then ...
If the little brother had not wanted candy, then ...
If the father had told the big brother not to go, then ...
If the mother had not let the big brother visit his father,
       then ...

If the big brother had not gone to get candy, then ...
If the pursuer had followed the dispatcher's order, then ...
If the young man had not talked to the pursuer, then ...
If the young man had not been wearing a hoodie, then ...
Dare I say if the young man had not been black?

Flashback almost ten years to all of the boy warriors.
Flashback almost fifty years to a young man who
       whistled.
Flashback almost 250 years to a young man out
       looking for wood to make a drum.
Flashback more than 2000 years when a troubled king
       decreed boys age two and under to be slain.

How many times have how many boys been killed for so
       little?
Is there anything to be said or done?

All the ifs in all the world will negate not one killing nor
       capture just as all the thens in all the world will resurrect not one
       young man.

03/21/12

Relieving Pressure

There's a poem in my head.
It won't go away.
My head is not always a good place for a poem.
I try to push the poem aside, put it under whatever.
But it won't go away.
Sometimes I jot a word or two as I drive.
Other times I have to pull over to the side of
the road and complete an idea.
Sentences scribbled in church, notes scrawled on playbills,
A line from a TV show, a quote from a sage or
six-year-old,
A response to a question, a question raised by
a response—any can be the spark for a poem.

Occasionally I can't sleep.
I write by the light of the Mac.
But more and more I have to turn on the light, grab the Mac, make the words
visible.
Snatches become complete when there's a poem on paper, when I relieve the
pressure,
when I can get the poem out of my head.

03/26/09

Freedom—Or the Lack Thereof

Time
Geography
Genetics
Genes
Birth Order
Metabolism
Heritage
Society
Education
Exposure

All of the above infringe on our freedom—
not always, of course,
not to the same degree, of course.
Bound, hampered, inextricably connected,
So much of this stuff over which we have little or no control diminishes our freedom.
Yet the freest among us know to take what we have and make what we want.
And some of us do, some of us do.

03/08/11

Suggestions

Go along to get along.
A half loaf is better than none.
A bird in the hand is worth two in the bushes.
To all I say—maybe or sometimes.
Do you go along with the bank robber or drunk driver?
Do you want the loaf with mold?
Do you want to keep the bird with a disease?
Watch use of "all" and "always" and "never."
Weigh.
Consider.
Scrutinize.

Options. Options. Options.
Neither be prodded nor paralyzed.
Know the options.
Choose well.

03/14/11

How Much?

Smidgeon,
Dash,
Pinch
Tad,
How much is too much?
Or too little?
What is "just right"?

Goldilocks may be the only one who knows.

Too little discipline or too much discipline = bad
Too little attention or too much attention = bad

So once again we may err because we cannot always tell how much is enough.

12/29/10

Memory, What We Remember

Tapes.
I used to think only the elderly had what I label head tapes,
conversations repeated to all who listen.

Now I know we all have head tapes.
I know the tapes generally shorten with age.
Reels, 78's, 33's, 45's, eight tracks, cassettes, cd's, MP3's,
DVD's—the length is the greatest variable.

Accomplished achievements
                    and perceived achievements
Crimes perpetrated against us
                    and perceived crimes against us
Real wounds
        and imagined wounds

            And there's also space for the person spoken to:
            How are you? How's your sister? What are you doing?

Soon, however, the content returns to where it began.
The testimonies remain about the same, almost verbatim.

            Again we hear accomplished achievements
                    and perceived achievements
Crimes perpetrated against us
                    and perceived crimes against us
Real wounds
        and imagined wounds.

12/27/10

Reassessment

Maybe he couldn't fix it but didn't want to say he
        couldn't.
Maybe he had failed too many times.
So he was more comfortable doing nothing.
Maybe he was afraid.
Maybe he didn't know how.
Maybe he just didn't want to because he learned
        fixing one something often leads to fixing
        another.
Perhaps he was familiar with slippery slopes and slip
        sliding.

He knew whatever the cause, so much is not as it appears.

Vow to consider other possibilities for one's
        unsatisfactory response, especially the
        possibility of which you are most certain.

07/20/11

A Standstill

I did not yell.
Neither did they.

I did not cry.
Some of them did.

My voice did not crack.
My hands did not shake.

I answered every question,
Elaborated when necessary,
Explained further if asked.

I never backed down.
I never lied,
Said exactly what I meant.

And still we were on opposite sides.

We could have gone longer.
I could have presented more evidence.
They could have tried harder to convince.
But neither side was going to budge.
For them, logic took a vacation a long time ago.
This was no time to reintroduce it.
For me, emotion should have been excused.
The subject is too important to be clouded by nice.
What each side saw the other could not.

Time would have to reveal the truth.
Time can do that.

One question: what's the minority or majority to do
while waiting for the other side to see the
revelation?

04/11/11

Obscenity

Deplorable, disgusting, inhumane, reprehensible,
        unacceptable say some.
Urinating on the dead is obscene.
Of course, it is!
All cultures agree, especially the citizens not in the fray.
But so are scalping, impaling body parts and bodies:
        displays which supposedly say I am better
            in actuality lessen, reduce, diminish the perpetrator.
All is desecration.
And yet these cultures continue to send persons,
        generally young persons, to war.

Destruction of cultures, their landmarks, artifacts that
        belong to humans everywhere, this too is obscene.
More obscene is the maiming and mutilating of bodies,
        minds, and hearts.
More obscene are all of the childless parents and
        parentless children, all of the persons with no spouse,
        no mates, no buddy because of war.
Most obscene are all of the countries not designating war
        obscene.

And what I wonder is when will the same cultures
        screaming obscene over urinating on dead bodies
        scream as vehemently over war being obscene.

With such a beginning perhaps we can end this most gross
        obscenity.

01/17/12

Twins Born at Different Times

Twin I.

He killed his wife.
He molested children.
They were robbing her husband.
They wanted to make money.
She demanded a divorce.
She loved her boyfriend who wanted her childless.

Though oblivious to the consequences, all destroyed lives to satisfy their selfishness.
Doubtlessly they believed they did what they had to do?
Surely the loss of the criminal is not in vain.
Surely.

03/24/11

Twin II.

                        He saved his wife.
                      He protected a stranger.
                      They were serving their country.
                      They wanted to give away Bibles.
                      He rescued fellow airline passengers.
                      He ran into a burning house to save his mom.

Though perhaps not their intention, all gave their lives to save the lives of others.
                Doubtlessly they believed they did what they had to do.
                      Surely losing them is not in vain.
                            Surely.

Both twins are humans, both a compilation of experiences.
Similarities we do not always see or consider exist.
We wring our hands.
We dwell on the differences.
Meanwhile, more perpetrators perpetrate and more life
    savers save.

02/28/11

Obstacles

I don't tackle all obstacles.
I do not believe in wasting energy.
Some obstacles I leave alone.
Others obstacles I go around.
Some obstacles I stare down.

But there are obstacles outside the
        above realms.
I have to decide which way to go, where to
        go, what to do.
These obstacles cause me to act.
They may alter me drastically, devastate or
        eradicate me momentarily or longer, much longer.

To save myself I have to act.
Speak. Stand. Shout, if necessary.
Sometimes stop works.
Other times I must speak and stand.
Making obstacles bigger is not my goal.
Managed or eliminated obstacles is my goal.

03/16/11

A Bio

For the woman who told me she had no bio…

Everybody has a bio.
Take yourself, for example.
You've been here a while.
You've seen something.
You've done something.

You do something well.
You do something often.

You're a member of something.

What statement is your guide?
What's your operating principle?
How did it get to be?
What's your mission?
Who has helped you?
Whom have you helped?
What's your greatest success?
What's your proudest moment?

Go ahead.
Share a bit of your story.
You have one, and it needs to be told.
No one at all times sees situations exactly as you do.
No one can tell your story as you do.

03/15/11

Escapists

No decreasing eyesight
No waning hearing
No dentures
No foods denied
No cane, walker, or wheelchair

No forfeited driver's license
No destination off limits

No Parkinson's nor ALS
No Alzheimer's nor dementia

No fear of leaving home
No fear of losing home
No detesting a nursing home
No more being misunderstood
No more misunderstanding
No more disappointments
No more betrayals—imagined or real:

They beat so many assaults flesh is heir to
because The Grim Reaper got to them early.

03/28/11

There Is No Half-Time

There is no half-time in life.
There is no seven-inning stretch, intermission, or hiatus.
There is no pause, time out, or interlude.
There is no spring or winter break, certainly no summer vacation.
The sooner we know the clock "runs" steadily at the same pace, regardless of our action or
inaction, the better.
We may do less or more, move or not, but our
taking a break does not stop, slow, or speed the clock.
The time flying for one may be time creeping for another.
How can that be?
Easily.
Reminders of our finiteness are all around.
We may choose to acknowledge or not, scoot or straggle, but there is no half-time.

Inspired by Adam Korpak's *There Is No Half-Time*   *03/20/12*

What She Has Become

You think it's sad seeing a loved one with dementia?
Sadder is seeing a loved one who knows she has
    dementia.
Family and friends she knows so much about.
She knows thoughts come.
But rarely are they the thoughts she needs at the moment.
Nothing comes when she needs something.
Forgetting how to add, subtract, multiply, and divide,
Telling the same story without knowing the listener has
    heard it countless times,
Remembering this face but not another known as well,
She can describe her fifty-year-old daughter's birthday
    party when the daughter was five as if it were yesterday but some days
    can't remember the daughter.
Other days to her granddaughter is this daughter.
Most days she knows her beloved sister.
Sometimes when she is right, she hesitates because she
    thinks she is wrong.
A body healthy in all but one sense is controlled by a
    brain that fails inspection.
A once exceptionally confident woman no longer can
    define the word *confidence*.
She is uncertain, hesitant, apprehensive.
These previously alien words now inhabit her brain.
They paralyze her brain not her body.

Friends and family can see her but can't help reflecting on
        the person they knew.
Once again a glorious being goes out with a bang or
        whimper, both signifying nothing.
The only help for those remaining is yet another reminder
        that sometimes this is as it is.

03/24/11

From Like to Dislike

I like him because he thinks critically.
He speaks articulately.
He listens attentively.

I dislike him because
He thinks of mean, cruel ways to hurt.
He speaks to belittle and berate.
He listens so he can vilify.

Gradually he moved from my like to my dislike list.
We converse, but not the same.
He, disappointingly, has yet to observe.
Guarding every word every time is tiring,
Wishing I could return to ignorance futile.
Movement from not knowing to knowing can be painful
despite the benefit.
And knowing he feels compelled, is compelled (?) to act as he
does makes me not consider cutting ties.

02/28/11

No Boots on the Ground

"No boots on the ground," said the President.
Thus far, HISTORY, maybe not American History, but
        HISTORY has recorded differently.
But Yemen, Libya, Somalia—all will be different.
"No boots on the ground," say our leaders.
So often boots on the ground is the American Way.
All of those warnings about entangling alliances and
        a military industrial complex appear to mean almost
        nothing to folks in control.
Oh, they'll say how a body died for his or her country,
        how being in harm's way and mutilated or killed
        as a result is the only way to protect our rights,
        protect the rights of the natives, give them our brand
        of democracy, give them what we know they want
        and need.
But to succeed the American Way, we often have boots
        on the ground.
It is the boots of the leaders and decision
        makers that will not be on the ground.
There is never a question, a discussion of whose boots
        will be on the ground.
But honestly, there are times when rather than boots we
        have shoes on the ground, shoes that do not belong to
        the leaders and decision makers.

05/30/11
revised 08/13/11

An Attempt at Humor

A policeman, behind her?
More than forty years and no ticket!
But she instinctively knew a ticket was coming.
"Where," said the officer, "are you going?"
"To a meeting, a very important meeting," was the answer.
She had left home later than planned.
The snow scared her.
She was ready at least an hour ahead of time.
But the computer said snow and ice, and she always said no to snow and ice
when it was on the street, especially when she was home.
Instead of leaving 2½ hours early as planned, she was leaving two hours late.
This was an important meeting; people were counting on her, some very proud
of her.
But there was the snow.
When she saw for herself, the computer was wrong, she felt better, drove faster.
Somewhere she put on this cd—her favorite cd because it had been made
especially for her.
She didn't just like the songs; she loved the songs.
But she could not divulge this information to the officer
who could tell there was no alcohol or drugs.
She certainly had not been driving recklessly.
But he had to give her a ticket; she was first tracked from the air at 73 mph,
only three miles
over the limit.
But this last time—well, he showed her.
He had to give her a ticket, and yes, the insurance company would know; this
is a moving
violation.

                    God, please.
But she had no defense; she had exceeded the speed limit.
She honestly did not know how much she had exceeded
            the speed limit.
But she could not tell the officer the real reason—reasons.
The officer was a young man.
He could not understand that she was listening to sermons
            by Al, Marvin, Junior, Jackie... a ballad by Ray.
And there was Otis; Otis might have been the one most
            responsible; she believes in tenderness.
On second thought, it could have been Osborne and
            company.
But Aretha could bear the blame; there's no comparison
            to a woman's feeling like a natural woman, and Aretha understands.
Martha, however, must also bear some of the blame.
Streets around the world have been the scene for all kinds
            of dancing to Martha's singing.
The speeder herself had been dancing to it since 1962,
            yes, 1962 when she was a mere child; from
            Grambling, Louisiana, to Beijing, China, she had
            danced to it.
She could never be still while listening to Martha, even
            when she consciously made the effort not to move.
But after more thought, she concluded the blame falls
            squarely on the shoulders of the Temptations!
That David Ruffin, he's the one: "My Girl," the song that
            tops all kinds of lists all of the time. But this woman
            has substituted "God" for "Girl" since college days.

Try it.
No human can sustain such a feeling for very long, but....
Well, it was probably those guys.
All that snow on the side of the road and not on the
  freeway just made her drive faster and faster and
  faster.
Any sane person of a certain age could have been carried
  away for concentrating on any one of those
  spokespersons!
But the listener had all of these songs, one following the
  other, repeated at her discretion, two, three times!
No harm was done to anyone but the listener.
She still can't believe it.
But when the insurance is increased, she'll remember
  where the real blame lies—with those singers!
She would never drive that fast without being under the
  influence of those singers.
And you need to know that this would not have happened
  had not all of those particular folks been singing their
  hearts out.
No, any one of them could not have made her do this.
It was the combination, all of these inimitable singers are
  responsible for that ticket and maybe the person who
  made the cd.
She was just driving, directing the vehicle.
She never saw the speedometer at 93.

August 2011

The Hand and Time

The trembling hand usually goes unnoticed.
Not so lately.
Pause to pick up a pill or push a button.
Performing neither is terrible.
What is terrible is the once beautiful handwriting
    now unreadable sometimes by readers and the
    writer.
What was for years intermittent shaking is now
    sometimes uncontrollable shaking.
Rather than the letters the brain selected, the hand leads
    the pen to make chicken scratch.
Alas, one more reminder of time winding down...
One can only pray that the brain does not soon follow
    suit.

4/11/11

Vows Broken

The wedding vows really sound good.
But I can truly see why so many of us break them.
I can see why so many couples thoughtfully and intentionally exclude obey.
As brides and grooms promise to be faithful and true, they usually mean it.
They certainly believe they can love, comfort, and keep
each other.
They sincerely believe they can forsake all others as long as they both shall live.
They honestly believe they can all their worldly goods
endow.
They positively believe they can stay together in sickness and in health, in poverty or in
wealth,
'til death do them part.
Some folks can and do or routinely give the impression
they do.
However, what they learn after the union sometimes trumps what they previously
knew.
And so they sometimes regretfully—or gleefully—break
the vows made to each other, family, friends,
society, and God.
Some definitely believe God understands.
It is those near the couple and one party of the couple who often do not understand.

02/25/11

MUSINGS

The Help

Helping does not always mean doing something.
Sometimes helping is doing absolutely nothing.
Sometimes helping is listening.
Still other times helping is speaking.
Wise is the individual who knows when to do which
      and what help means when.

05/13/09

Excuses

"I know she's on meds," she said.
Really?
"I can tell.
She has that look.
She's here but faraway."
What's your excuse, I wanted to ask.

05/26/10

The Quick and the Dead

Just in case we forget we're mortal, reminders from the Grim Reaper come
more often and
more noticeably.
Job: man that is born of a woman is of few days
and full of trouble.
Shakespeare: we ripe and ripe and then we rot
and rot.
How few those days are!
How quickly this rotting begins!

06/03/10

Limits

Because the O-rings on the space-bound Challenger's solid rocket booster
could withstand just so much pressure

And the rivets of the unsinkable Titanic
could withstand just so much pressure,

Why don't more people see that our little built-to-fail
bodies can withstand just so much pressure?

We have limits…not the same limits, but limits
nevertheless.

02/16/11

Familiarity

Initially, I said, "It's wrong to say familiarity breeds contempt."
Later I said, "Familiarity does not necessarily breed contempt."
Eventually I grew to say, "Ok. Sometimes familiarity breeds contempt."
Now I see almost always familiarity breeds contempt.

02/25/11

Mind and Matter

I believe in mind over matter.
It works for me, almost always.
But sometimes the matter overwhelms the mind.

03/11

Words

If you love me...
If you had a backbone...
What follows these two clauses have gotten more
      folks in more trouble than any words I know...
Unless I consider the phrases law and order and for
      the good of the country.

02/06/12, 02/09/12

Windmills—Or Not

A windmill deemed a windmill is not always one, just
as something deemed not a windmill may very
well be one.
One person's windmill may be another's dream
materialized.
We can't always tell at the beginning of the
adventure.
And we can't always trust folks who know or see
earlier than we do.
Obviously we do not know and see the same.
Clearly we do not interpret the same.
We just do what we do, sometimes good and other times
not so good, sometimes negative and other times positive.

03/04/11

Letting Someone In

Beware of letting a person in.
Child, parent, sibling, or friend—beware.
Make no eye contact.
Look at a needy person, and you may help,
become blinded to flaws.
So beware of letting a person in.
Once in, a person may take brain, lungs, heart.
Your mind may become saturated,
Your lungs deoxygenated,
Your heart asphyxiated.
No contact is a sure fire way to lessen personhood.
Then blindness, mindlessness, breathlessness, and
heartlessness set in.
You may have to resort to shoving someone out.
Sad as this may be, not shoving may mean being shoved, shoved out simply
because you let someone in.

02/22/11

Observation

There is nothing in the world like observation.
Observing is so much more than seeing.
An observer does more than see.
The observer identifies, describes, categorizes the small picture, the big picture
and much that is in between:

Details
Angles
Sides
Perspectives
Parts
Surface
Depth
Whole

The observant one gets busy
Remembering
Organizing
Connecting
Theorizing
Analyzing
Synthesizing.

Then the best observers share their observations.

03/10/11

Being Slow

Sometimes, there's something to be said about being slow.
There is indeed a time to take time.
Remember the tortoise beating the hare,
And the Pointer Sisters wanting a slow hand,
Alcoholics Anonymous saying one day at a time
The Bible reminding God is slow to anger.

Eat slowly.
Take your time.
There's a time to take time, sometimes.

Not Enough Time

There's not enough time for every wealthy person to see the value of ending poverty.
There's not enough time for every incarcerated innocent person to be exonerated.
There's not enough time to assure each guilty person is defended legally and punished fairly.
There's not enough time for every bureaucrat to see the value of education.
There's not enough time for everyone to see the sexism in choices.
There's not enough time for everyone to see the folly of trickery.
There's not enough time for every boss to go undercover.
There's not enough time for every racist to see his or her racism.
There's not enough time for every one to get everything deserved.

There's just not enough time, resources, or energy
for the media, organizations, communities (civil or
legal), to eradicate all the wrong.

Worse, there's the problem of not seeing the same.
With the same evidence, we don't always draw the same conclusions.
What the world needs is an invention that gets a critical mass to recognize quickly the good and then spread the good and stamp out the bad.
Can we work on that?

12/30/10

Flags

He signed up for the red, white, and blue,
Let some clown convince him he was fighting for his
country, protecting the American way of life.
(I think the Afghans, Iraqis, all insurgents, etc. would say they are fighting for
their way of life.)
He fought against the red, white, black, and green.
Counterparts had told them they were fighting for their
country too.
It did not take long before those around him saw all flags as
red.
Behavior was the first obvious sign of change—but
only after he saw comrades wounded or killed not once or twice but at least
three times.
He came home where people who knew him saw red flags
everywhere.
Drinking, drinking while driving
Abusing drugs—none was the least bit characteristic of
him.

But then, he was no more; he had become someone else.
Deserting the place he volunteered to be,
Threatening the folks with whom he wanted to be.
One day as certain as suicide bombers aimed and struck, he
dressed for war and waited for the police to carry out
his suicide.
The police obliged.

02/15/11

Few Corrections

Every error does not need correcting.
There are times I want to whisper, "That's not the way it was."
I want to say, "You don't have all the information; you don't have enough information."
I want to explain, "It did not happen that way."
I want to confide, "I was there."
I want to reveal, "I have the whole story, conversed with both parties."
Other times I want to scream some of those lines.
Usually, I keep quiet.
I keep quiet because I wish to keep the peace.
I keep quiet because every error does not need correcting.
I keep quiet because so often so many of us believe what
we want to believe, regardless of the facts.

12/27/10

Choices

One can pick and choose but not everywhere all of the
time.
Falklands, Israel, Suribachi,
Iraq, Iran, Somalia:
We must choose wisely when we get to choose.
Armed with the best information, we don't always choose
the best
mates, neighborhoods, schools, jobs, cars, churches,
treatment.
But always there are consequences:
some we know;
some we expect;
and those we could never have expected.

The Photographer Artist

In a world where so often humans can control so little, the
        photographer artist gets to control more more often.
Choose the film.
Consider a filter.
Pick any angle.
Decide where to stand, sit, or lie.
Add or subtract color or none.
Show a black sky as easily as a blue one.
Accent a pattern.
Take any part of a whole.
Use the part as the whole.
Make the subject unrecognizable for most.
Give the audience what you want.
Let them take it or leave it.

Function is the foremost feature for the artist architect.
Construction, whether for a concert hall or court house,
        bridge or library, is the domain, the concern of the
        contractor artist.
The photographer artist controls, owns the little
        photography.

Function and form appear thrown to the wind.
Actually, masterpieces rest squarely on what emerges from
        the artist's combination of function and form.
Thus a segment of a mammoth three-dimensional creation
        may become the subject of a significantly smaller two-dimensional
        creation of a different kind as likely as a minute creation may become
        gargantuan.

11/14, 17/05 ??   Inspired by Thomas Ager's *Tokonoma Lucida-Rohatsu*

Chaos

Chaos?
What chaos?
The sun "rises."
The sun "sets."
(We know the sun does not move.)
Years have twelve months,
365 days, except what we call a leap year.
Days have twenty-four hours.
Hours have sixty minutes.
Minutes have sixty seconds.
The crocuses, narcissuses come up, matchless beauty.
And yet, in no time, it seems, they die.
Rain comes down, more or less than we want or need, but it comes down.
Hail and snow do the same.
Meteorologists predict, accuracy steadily improving it seems.
But they do not produce any of that weather they sometimes seem to claim.
The earth keeps spinning.
No amount of our action or inaction affects this spinning.
People are born everyday; people die everyday.
So, where is the chaos?
Granted, there's much that distracts, disappoints, and destroys.
But real chaos, I sometimes fear, we have yet to see.
The Creator does, indeed, have the world in His hands.

03/12/09

Not Always Possible

No!
Stop it!
Don't say it!
It is not true!

I don't care how sincere you are.
Your wealth and power mean little here.

You can't always protect me.
You can't always be there for me.
You can't always be here for me.

I wish you could.

But thanks for wanting to protect me.
Thanks for trying to protect me.
Just knowing you want to, that you'll try to, makes everything easier.

02/24/10

My Head Tapes

As near as I can tell—and a faithful listener may tell
Better—my head tapes are related to these subjects: time (rarely a friend), randomness (prevalence), information (use and abuse), truth (whole), endurance (varied strength),
fairness (irrelevance)
education (misuse), travel (revelations).
Arcing and undergirding all of these is the oft repeated do unto others as you would have them do unto you.

Cane's mom died giving birth to him; Moss's mom
is in her nineties.
Clarice had twelve babies and abandoned them all;
Creola spent more than twelve years trying to conceive one baby—and never did.
Fiddler was born a slave and died a slave, resigned to
his fate.
Faith was born with all the freedom money
can provide and accomplished nothing.
Examples abound.
My tapes influence every action and inaction.
But recognizing them makes negotiation through the maze of life easier, not easy, but
easier.

03/24/11

Things to Do

Tasks to do
Food to eat
Folks to greet
Plays to view
Pieces to write
Trips to take
Books to read
Works to print
Music to hear
Vistas to see
Problems to solve

Ignore the always neutral clock.
It's ticking, always ticking.
It's neither fast nor slow.
Go.
Just do.

12/29/10

Why?

A civic association
A nursing home
Workplaces
Post offices, above average
College campuses
High school campuses
McDonald's
Houses

All settings for mass killings, some more than others.
Victims random sometimes,
Family, friends, bosses other times.
Not one perpetrator suffered an unheard of
once-in-a-lifetime ailment.
Rejection, frustration, disappointment, loss, illness,
Stress—all of us humans who live a while
experience such to varying degrees.
Envy, jealousy, pain, failure, loneliness—all of
us experience these too.
Yet no one can explain why some of us
respond by hurting others and/or self and
some of us respond by being kinder
and/or gentler.
Was it post-traumatic stress?
Was there an accumulation of molehills?
Was there one mountain too many?
Was there no preparation for disaster?

Was it overwhelming tiredness?
Was it something added or subtracted,
too little or too much?
Was there something someone could have done?

04/06/09

The Subjectivity of Objectivity

Objective.
Let's be objective.
How often does that command make a point the point?
Consider.
Truth—objectivity is always subjective:
This president or not
This pastor or that
This pipeline or not
PTSD or not
This highway/tunnel or not
More gun laws or not
Birth control or not
Abortion or not
Charter schools or not
Islam or not
Christianity or not
War or not.
Add your subjects.
Both sides accuse the other of not being objective.
Both sides are convinced the other is not looking at the
        facts.
A third party may think neither side wants to be confused
        with facts.
Can both sides be right?
Both list plusses and cons, one's plus often being the
        other's con.
More and more objectivity seems to have its roots in
        subjectivity.

03/17/12

The Paradox of Handling

"It's in your hands," the theys of the world say often.
The theys say, "Open your hands and let go or close and
    crush."
The theys seem not to know about the gradations between
    opening and closing, don't know the hand has to be open or closed, a
    little, a lot, or somewhere in between all the time.
This sounds simple, not the least cumbersome.
But in reality, the number of times holding too tightly and
    destroying unwittingly plus the times squeezing
    knowingly and destroying equally makes murderers of us all.
Being in our hands is not necessarily good.
On as many occasions we've held too loosely and
    wrought destruction.
We released that we could have had if only we'd held on
    a bit or destroyed something or someone because we
    refused to exert the required pressure.
Like much of life, the hand dream can be a hand
    nightmare because there's no great Hand Holder to
    tell us how tightly or loosely to hold.
Once again, we face the Great Dilemma: with the best of
    information we may destroy or be destroyed.
We seem destined to fail, yet most of us most of the time
    feel our way forward, forever handling never knowing how much
    force, pressure is enough or too much.
Pause, if we like, but the world keeps spinning—with or
    without us.
Hands open or closed, Life—not always as we know it or
    want it or like—goes on.
And the best nor the fittest always survive.

08/06/04

It's a Wrap

Sometimes—and don't misunderstand.
Sometimes be the reason as huge as global interconnectedness, technological innovations, or population increase or as small as he said/she said, the kid, pet, plant, or vehicle was or wasn't mine, the best response is, "It's a wrap."

03/16/12

I Ask Why

Some people never ask why.
Best friend accidentally shoots
a healthy nineteen-year-old who becomes a paraplegic
A wife a man loves leaves him for his brother
A husband a woman loves leaves her for her best friend
A sister tells her sister don't come to her funeral
A woman has ovarian cancer then brain cancer
A woman has three surgeries in three weeks
A woman drives 1200 miles to a wedding because she's afraid to fly—on the
return trip a
wrong-way driver hits her head-on
A brilliant professor shrinks away with Parkinson's
A woman's parents die in a house fire—locked in by steel doors they installed
to protect themselves
A man marries Sunday, has a fatal heart attack the following Wednesday
A man witnesses the death of his three daughters and a niece—and still believes
there can be
peace in Israel
The list could go on and on.
Many say they never ask why.
But I do!
Almost always.
"Why?"

03/04/11

A Patch of Ground

Shakespeare should know folks are still fighting over a patch of ground,
A patch too small for a grave for each.
And yet they fight.
Still they fight.
There have always been fighters,
And it seems there will always be fighters:
Those who willingly fight at all costs
for God, country, family, honor.
They fight, they change and are changed, they die or are dead.

There have always been those who desperately want not to fight, recoil at fighting.
"Let others have the land," they say.
The cost to fight is too high.
"We won't pay," they say.

There have always been those in the midst who call for
reason, morality, life—those who see the futility of war,
those who know everyone loses but some lose more,
so much more than others.

On both sides and for those in the middle, ones loved are lost.
Too bad such losses are not enough to stop the madness.

12/28/10

Molehills Becoming Mountains

So often so little lays the foundation for an argument,
a sometimes shallow or weak foundation, but a foundation still.
Sure, it should not be.
But it is what it is.
Disagreements originate and other times accumulate.
One did not hear—did not physically hear.
Forget understand!
Simply: One did not hear what the other said!

How can they possibly not be at odds?
How can anyone be sure another is heard?
Heard correctly?
What can we do to avoid mishearing?
All we can do is listen intently.
We can ask the speaker to repeat.
Of course, we then risk being labeled inattentive.
What are we to do?
All I can say is try harder and be more patient.
Neither will eliminate all problems, but the number of problems will be reduced.

11/25/10

Brainprint

Fingerprint
Footprint
Voiceprint
No one argues about these.
What about a brainprint?
Not just an image of the brain but every action of the brain.
Each of us has a unique brain.
No brainprint is better than another, but each is different.
Perhaps brainprint difference explains the confusion so often present, confusion which arises in the least likeliest places, confusion which no one intended.

Perhaps this explains why no one ever understands everything we say.
Perhaps this is why though facing the same situation, some fight, some flee, some adapt, others die.
Some cling to home regardless; others migrate regardless.
Some travel thousands of miles without maps; others get lost in their neighborhoods.
Some endure destructive relationships; others escape at the first hint of confusion.

Some love figurative language and use it often;
others abhor figurative language, use it
sparingly, and understand it rarely.
Some have to teach; others never knowingly
teach.
Some can repair anything; others nothing.
Some suffer indignities repeatedly; others deem
one indignity too much.
What if being a visual, auditory, or kinesthetic
learner plays a smaller role than generally
thought?
What if age, circumstance, environment, or
race—any of the many categories we use to
distinguish one of us from another—plays a
smaller part than we know?
What if the overriding factor is the brainprint
over which we have no control?

11/17/10

Beliefs

Some see a mirage for what it is.
Others exhaust themselves—and those around them—ttrying to make that mirage an oasis.
Some try to make a silk purse out of a sow's ear.
Some try to get blood from a turnip.
Some try to get bread from a stone.
All of this stuff we were told couldn't be done
some of us believed; others didn't believe.
and this has made all the difference,
positive OR negative.

12/28/10

Special Songs

"I love to praise Him.
I love to praise Him."
I do not know when the song came,
what made it come.
But every Sunday morning in the shower, there it would be.
For years the song came.
I eventually stopped trying to determine how it came.
I just enjoyed the voice singing those words.
The whole song would "play" and then repeat,
"I love to praise Him.
I love to praise Him."

And then one day, years after I first noticed the recurring song,
there was no song!
Sunday after Sunday there was no song.
I missed it.
But it would not come.
I ached for it.

As suddenly as it left one day it was back!
Oh, I was happy, again.
Baffled but happy.
One Sunday it was there; then it disappeared.

Eventually I forgot it wasn't there.

Then one Sunday—always Sunday—there was a new song.
It had come as suddenly and as mysteriously as the other.

"Jehovah Jireh, my provider…"
Pleased, I was.
The song came three times.
And then it was gone, as suddenly as it had come.
This morning I woke up to another song:

"Mama Told Me Not to Come."
From where did it come?
I don't know any other words.
I don't know the meaning.
But the words wouldn't go away.
The words are making me write.
Can someone explain?

03/06/11

The Nastiest Word

What's the nastiest word you know?
"Segregation" for me...

Doctors' offices
Water fountains
Hospitals
Neighborhoods
Restrooms
Schools
Colleges
Universities
Restaurants
Staircases
Courtrooms
Parks
Sports
Taxis
Mortuaries
Movie theaters
Beauty salons
Barber shops
Parking lots
Night clubs

Detention centers
Bus stations
Train depots
Cemeteries

The world did not operate better because races
> were separate.
But generations paid and pay horrendous prices
> because races were separate.
Descendants of the segregationists regularly scorn those
> poor, homeless, unskilled, uneducated, sick
> descendants of the segregated without ever
> seeing a connection between then and now.
> (Some say the segregationists do see and are driven to destroy what
> they see!)
Segregation, Jim Crow—despite the decades—
> continues to affect and influence visibly and
> invisibly in ways courts cannot always
> correct and quite often do not see.
No, I can think of no word as nasty as "segregation."

But I must admit the word "integration" is not nearly as
> nice as I thought it would be.

2010

Maggots

I saw a maggot today.
Actually I saw many, thousands maybe.
I couldn't remember when I had last seen one.
Never thought about them.
Yet, there they were.
Move, move, move.
All over the place, all over each other,
Never still,
Move, move, move.
I do not know what occupied them,
Only that they worked rapidly, feverishly.
I daresay intently moved.
It had been decades since I saw a maggot.
A helpful friend had put scraps in a plastic bag,
placed it on my deck.
I discovered the bag a week later, deposited it
in the covered garbage can—in the sun.
I came out a few days later to discover maggots
everywhere!
Couldn't help thinking how those little maggots
were dining on what once was a big pig or
cow.
Couldn't help thinking how we in all of our
sophistication and complexity, supposed
superiority could, can, will—embalming fluid, fire, or water not interfering—
indeed be food
for
maggots.

09/21/10

Innocent Eggs

Not eggs.
Eggs were not responsible for the murder.
Husband or wife could've been physically ill.
Mental illness could've been the culprit.
Maybe one of them was having an affair.
More may have been required of Mom and Dad.
Perhaps one demanded a divorce.
Somebody could have been jobless.
Maybe there was not enough money.
Stress has at least a thousand entrances but not so many exits—at least exits that we see.

Nobody knows what he had borne for how long.

Now, the eggs might be responsible for a headache.
But, like the straw accused of breaking the camel's back, the eggs got a raw deal.
No, eggs were not the reason for the murders.
Believe me: eggs were not the reason.

An East Coast man killed five and then himself; the same week a West Coast refugee killed her son-in-law, two granddaughters, and herself and wounded another family member. (It was not the eggs nor anything else so simple.)

09/25/10

I Wish ...

I wish I could save the sea turtles, wolves, polar bears, and whales,
stop gerrymandering
make all candidates good
fund all of the good causes—be they artistic,
medical, social, legal, religious, environmental, political
provide all children with loving, knowledgeable moms and dads
Heal the sick
House the homeless
End trafficking of every kind
Eliminate the need for a catcher in the rye
Stamp out disease and hunger and loneliness too
Terminate war for everyone everywhere for evermore
Educate everyone—first teaching them to think critically
and categorically proving the value of critical thinking.
However, money, skill, initiative, talent, strength,
and time too often elude me.
I am thus relegated to save whom and what I can
with what I have when I can.
No one would demand more.
Right?

10/08/10

Terror Colors

So now, the government rates terror risk.
One more result of 9/11.
Bin Laden won.
Something, it seems, will cost forever.
Severe Red
High Orange
Elevated Yellow
Guarded Blue
Low Green
Watch.
Be careful now.
Never mind how long the alerts alert.
nor that these flags may be as useful as duck and cover
during a nuclear attack.
Is terror always imminent?

P.S. The government began eliminating color-coded terror alerts January 27, 2011.

11/25/10

Georgia's Law

Explain the best you can.
But be prepared to be misunderstood.
Seriously.
Unfortunately, explaining more does not always solve
    the problem.
This is a principle.
No one makes you learn it in church or school,
    no Newton's Law or Golden Rule.
I want to help.
The sooner you learn this law, the better life gets.
So, here may be the best gift I can give you.
    Georgia's Law:
Explain the best you can;
But be prepared to be misunderstood.

03/12/11

Moving On

"I got to take it,"
Ostensibly he spoke of his medicine.
Actually he spoke of his dying.
He had to take it.
This journey ended or part of it did.
He did not want to linger.
But he did not want to die.
There were songs to sing, cd's to play,
programs to emcee, columns to write,
conversations to have, errands to run,
clothes to buy and return, rooms and a car to clean.
Most of all, there were kindnesses to show.
And he mentioned only the kindnesses.
Surprised at the magnitude and wealth of good
shown him, he desired to reciprocate,
extend similarly.
One lesson learned and reaffirmed from one who could do
no more: do all the good you can while you can.

09/01/10

Matt

The young man Matt was high, really high,
intelligent, confident, overachieving,
a medical doctor, engaged.
He was out with friends.
He was having a really good time.

And then he walked outside.

Still high, very high, Matt walked, smiled.

Then an idiot, a non-doctor, a never-would be
doctor, called Matt a _____
It was derogatory, a slur, a racial slur,
ignorance again at work.

And then
Matt, who was so high, so high,
intelligent, overachieving Matt did what he so often did.
He taught, or rather tried to teach, told the
ignorant one to cut the ignorance.
And the ignorant did what ignorance so often
does: lashed out physically because no mental acuity supports his point.

In an instant the known Matt became another Matt.
Who's there?
Despite his laurels, accomplishments, desire,
sincerity, determination, prayers even—
nothing could bring back the pre-Matt.

Oh, he made progress, returned to practice.
And then one day he went hiking, maybe to
clear his head, to attempt an escape from reliving that horrible moment when he
came
face to face with ignorance and evil, that terrible time which he tried not to relive
even
as daily his life evidenced the result of the ignorance and evil.

Now all we know is that he fell,
fell in some of the most beautiful scenery,
fell where nothing is neither for nor against us,
fell where only his ignorance—or maybe, maybe his intelligence—was responsible,
fell the final fall, the fall to his death.

07/03, 05/10

Opportunities

Opportunities define us, even when we miss them, maybe especially when we miss them.
So inopportunity, then, defines us too.
Equal opportunity sounds so good.
But when does it exist?
Where?
From birth to death there are opportunities.
No one can possibly take all of them.
Only one may be needed.
But which?
When?

And what do we do about opportunity gaps?

11/18/10

Lies

Lies.
Truth can be inconvenient
Inexpedient
Unbearable
Painful
Devastating
Life-threatening
Eye-opening.

So some resort to lies.
And lies may solve a problem temporarily,
Or may cause more problems
And may, on occasion, kill.

06/23/10

The Lie Continues

Leaders of countries, a handful of men, usually, lie.
They lie; they have lied for centuries.
This handful continue to say
and imply
"It is sweet and becoming to die for one's country."

A handful of men once again
send others, usually much younger men and
women, to fight.
They lure them with good and steady pay, tales of service,
camaraderie, honor.
(Is it so amazing that the poor and poor in spirit and esteem disproportionately answer
the call?)
They promise benefits some could never get if they didn't
risk everything by going to war.
Wrapped in the flag of a country, the handful
mouth hollow words.
Whether they believe the words is debatable.
A soldier has no way of knowing what values
will have to be put aside, that morality may
as well be dead.
The recognition of the lies is what so often kills
the soldier, kills mentally and or spiritually if not
physically.

The betrayal by persons believed and respected
is sometimes all that's needed to demoralize
and destroy the "warrior" placed on foreign
soil to protect God knows what.

———

According to Wikipedia's history about Viet Nam, "U. S. military advisors arrived beginning in 1950. U.S. involvement escalated in the early 1960s, with U.S. troop levels tripling in 1961 and tripling again in 1962. U.S. combat units were deployed beginning in 1965... Involvement peaked in 1968 at the time of the Tet Offensive. U.S. military involvement ended on 15 August 1973."

The United States launched attacks in Libya March 19, 2011. President Barack Obama and military officials say we will be out of Libya in "days." Muammar Gaddafi was captured October 20th and died soon afterwards. The U. S. withdrew. The North Atlantic Treaty Organization ended its military operations October 31st.

07/17/10, revised 10/08/10

Religion and Guns

They do cling to their guns and their religion.
That's not so bad.
Everybody clings to something:
Religion or guns,
Money, status,
Class, looks.
What's odd, say some, is the combination guns and religion.
But then that Bible they cling to says eye for an eye in the front and turn the other cheek in the back.
The clingers can be as contradictory as their Guide can be.

07/04/10

Art Interrupts

Artists make art all of the time, often against their will.
This urge has many names: creativity, ego, lust, agony,
      ecstasy, madness, depending on speaker and the reason for the speech.
Much goes not done and undone while artists are
      interrupted by what they have to do.
House, vehicle, yard, work—their day will come, but not
      while Art takes over.
Spouse, kids, other significant ones often must take a
      backseat to Art.
Sometimes as artists try their best to entertain loved ones,
      their mind is on Art.
Even when artists say, "I'll work a little while or an hour
      only" and really mean it, Art sometimes takes over and an hour becomes a day or more.
Artists KNOW they SHOULD be doing something
      else, but they have to get Art out of their head.
A painter's got to paint.
A sculptor's got to sculpt.
A writer's got to write.
There's no out.
A grocery bag, a fast food bag, an airline ticket or air bag,
      a utility bill, a newspaper, a napkin, a statement, a
      magazine page, anybody's flyer, a church bulletin, an
      art program, a Christmas card, that old standby
      envelope, any scrap of paper will do—at least temporarily.
Artists can be in the shower or on plane, bus, or train, on
      the sidewalk or in the swimming pool.

Art comes.

Art is often responsible for late meals and cold food.

Never paid or underpaid, artists continue to create their art.

(Overpaid is usually used only by people who don't understand the art nor realize what went into the creation.)

Their visions come to life, sometimes viewed and/or understood by them alone.

And, usually, they understand and see this as an interruption.

Artists know about interruptions.

So, notwithstanding, they go about the business of creating art.

But artists know and live with this fact: as Art becomes part of life, it interrupts.

Long live such interruptions!

05/08/06   Inspired by Thomas Ager's photograph *Haunted Noon*

Selected Stories

Stories, stories, stories.
Good ones, bad ones, happy and sad ones.
We're writing a story
Hearing a story
Telling a story
Beginning a story
In the middle of a story.
Finishing a story,
Always participating in a story—not always willingly.
Being left out can be part of the story.
We're the good, the bad, the ugly.
We're the protagonist or antagonist,
Flat or round
Dynamic or static
Maybe simply a stock character.
Other times we can only narrate.
Sometimes we control the action—to a degree.
Often we suffer the consequences of the action.
Usually we can't stop others from telling our stories,
Others who can get it so wrong—or right.
Ashamed of being fooled or having fooled,
Less than what we think we are or ought to be,
we never want to tell all the stories.
(I'll bet nobody wants to tell all of the stories.)
We tell selected stories.

06/23/10

Mama Nadi Confesses

I was not born Mama Nadi!
I was born a blank slate.
I had much written on me long before I could
speak or write.
Culture and Class wrote.
Parents wrote.
Place wrote.
Poverty wrote.
Pragmatism wrote.
Then War with its many negatives wrote.
War wrote longest and hardest, most indelibly and most brutally.
War ruined—boys and girls, men and women.
Rape wrote.
Rape ruined in a new way.
So now, I write, not necessarily when I want to write nor what I want to write.
But I write.
I came to be Mama Nadi!
No, I was not born Mama Nadi!

6/18/10 at Oregon Shakespeare Festival after seeing Lynn Nottage's drama *Ruined*

Promise Kept

They had dated.
They knew each other.
She was seventeen; he was eighteen.
So when the war came, he went.
But before he left, they got engaged.
When he returned, they married.
Each silently believed keeping one's word is of utmost importance.
So she did what she had to do.
He did the same.
And happiness was never part of their ever after.

May 2010

Soaring

What Icarus must have felt as he soared, actually flew,
was probably not alien to the Wright Brothers, Lindbergh, Earhart, Tuskegee
Airmen, or Yeager,
and certainly not to space travelers Shepard and Ride and
space walkers Armstrong and Harris.

Maybe the feeling was akin to what Armstrong must have felt when he walked
on the moon
or Peter felt as he walked on water.

Most of us have our feet on the ground most of the time.
Yet, there are those times when despite the physics we too soar.

And as often as possible, soaring ought to be part of the human condition.

05/16/10

Routine

Read Bible.
Get up.
Brush teeth.
Take pills.
Eat honey.
Eat breakfast.
Day after day after day,
Regardless of the day,
The routine begins the same.

Then come the variables.
Thank God for the variables.

Eat dinner.
Take pill.
Brush teeth.
Floss.
Lie down.
Thank God.

05/20/10

Real Mistakes

I made a mistake.
I was wrong.
I shouldn't have done it.
I take full responsibility.
My bad…

(Nothing—or so little—significantly changes
real mistakes, honesty notwithstanding.)

05/20/10

Dependent Clauses

If you love me…
If you had a backbone…
What follows these two clauses have gotten more
      folks in more trouble than any words I know…
          unless I consider the phrases law and order and for the good of the country.

02/09/12

Frogs and Princes

Some kids catch frogs, place them in a jar for no good reason.
After a few days, the frogs escape or are set free.
As far as we know, the frogs are not traumatized.

People catch people, place them in a jar for what they say is a good reason.
After a few days, years, or what seems like forever, the people escape or are set free.
Despite the length of capture, some people are traumatized, never to be the same.
Why would a frog want to be turned into a prince?

2/17, 25/11

The Problem with Memories

We remember pain and pleasure.
The incident could have transpired decades earlier, but we can often recall it as if it happened this morning.

No, we remember SOME pain and pleasure as if it happened this morning.
Other memories are not always so clear.
Rare is the memory that's photostatic.
Take, for instance, the night of the day of Mommy's funeral.
Did the Dad ask the kids to leave the house because he was provoked?
Or did the kids leave the house because they felt provoked?
Did the Dad do everything he could to get the Mother to the hospital?
Or did the Dad move exceptionally slow, warming up the car, for instance?
Why did Dad bypass the first hospital making his way to Charity Hospital?
Was this a conscious act?
Or did he head straight to the Charity Hospital where he had, until recently—been compelled to go?
All participants have their own memories, memories which can't be touched with truth or fiction.
Each of us is our record keeper.
Our skills vary from memory to memory and from time to time.

Sometimes we are better keepers of some memories than
    others involved in the memories.
Sometimes we can appeal to older siblings and relatives,
    friends, and neighbors.
Sometimes after hearing their truths—good, bad,
    intentional, incidental, accidental—we are forced to
    dismantle or discard.
And other times we ignore the facts, refuse to be confused
    with the facts.
We keep the original memory intact, or almost intact.
The cost is too high to change the memory.
But most of the time we are left to wonder, ponder what
    was, why, how.
Still we have the memory.
It belongs to us.
And depending on our abilities, we can make the memory
    What we thought it was or wanted it to be.

06/11/05

The Little Nothing Dress

Yes, I still have my little nothing dress, a. k. a. my little
    black dress.
I'll probably always have it.
Some might say the little dress is not what it used to be.
But Little Black Dress and I pay no attention.
We know we are better than we used to be.
Actually, the dress talks more than I do, so I'll just be
    quiet.

Thank you, Lady of the Dress. I know how shy you are.

"I am not as short as I used to be, but I cover more.
I don't go out as much as I used to.
Don't get me wrong.
I can dazzle.
I can move, love to move.
I can dance all night, dance every chance I get.
Remembering, forgetting, my lady and I can be the belle
    of the ball whether at a party with many or at home
    alone.

If I need to come off, I can.
I have never come off often.
And I come off less now.
I come off less because my Lady wants more.
Surely, you know, we prefer quality to quantity.
Just know that I come off at the right place, right pace, right
    time, and right reason.

And, of course, I do not come off for fools.

Yes, some may say I am not what I used to be.
But Lady and I don't mind.
In fact, we say Amen to that!
We are in better shape than we used to be.
We have no intention of going away.
The Lady and I really are like fine wine, the older the better.

Inspired by Susan Gans' painting *Little Nothing Dress*   2004

If You Lived Here ...

Nice house on a clean street.
Daddy manicuring the yard.
Mommy carrying in groceries,
Children playing.

All may look fine.
What could possibly be wrong?

Look more closely.
See the flames.

If you lived here, you would be on fire.
Your stomach would churn.
Nausea would play a major role in your life.
Your head would pound.
Your muscles would be taut.
Tense could always describe you.
You would think you were going to explode.
Food, Alcohol, Sex, Violence could become your best friend.

Here nobody says what needs to be said.
Here nobody can say what needs to be said.
And not saying what needs to be said can be deadly.
Ask Eric Harris and Dylan Klebold or Kip Kinkle.

Believe me when I say you do not want to live here.
If you lived here, flames would burn and possibly consume you.

10/14/05

Inspired by Jessica Dodge's painting
If You Lived Here You'd Already Be Home

Attention!

Skull and bones
A warning
A slap on a wrist
An alarm
A wake-up call

How many calls do we need?

More persons to die in streets without crosswalks
More miners to die in mines (or from ills contracted in the mines)
More drivers to be killed in unsafe vehicles
More plants and animals to absorb spilled oil

What is the tipping point?
Where is that 100th monkey?
How much makes a critical mass?

Generations have failed to heed all kinds of signs.
Too often humans trudge or run along making the same errors, getting the same results.
To avoid one more such death, we need a remedy.

Where is it?
When will it show up?
How long?
How much longer?

05/16/10

Michael

I want you back.
Just because we can never say goodbye, didn't say goodbye does not mean the eradication of separation.
I told you you can say "I'll be there" all you want, but you can't promise.
You can't know; nobody can.
The world holds too many unseen dangers.
No one can escape all of the dangers all of the time.
All you can do is hope and pray you'll be there.
You just can't promise.
Or, you can promise.
But the promise is near meaningless—
near because it usually makes you and the one getting the promise feel good.
But I know you've made a promise you may not be able to keep.
And not necessarily through no fault of yours.
As much as I want you to be there
There's no guarantee.
I told you, told you way back when that long
time ago when you first sang, "I'll be
there."
I told you you couldn't promise.
You may promise.
But for myriad reasons, you may be unable to keep your promise.

Began 06/27/09; completed 10/13/09

Sleep

"I want to sleep," said Michael.
"I need sleep."
He knew what he needed.
Sleep, something so natural, so easy for so many, something all animals need.
But sleep for Michael was murdered, indirectly by a soft
drink company and directly with drugs to fix the pain.
(I know people he trusted directed both moves.)

Of course, the soft drink company did not mean to harm Michael.
The soft drink owners wanted only to make money, and make more money.
And, Michael too, wanted to make more money.
Michael nor the soft drink company could never
Make/have enough money.
Yet all of that money could not buy sleep unless you consider paying a doctor
to prescribe the
Unprescribable ...
But Michael did get what he asked for: sleep, painless sleep,
restful sleep, nightmare-less sleep, uninterrupted sleep, just sleep.

05/26/10 & 06/15/10

Age

For me, there was no advent of ageing.
One day I couldn't find something.
I   could   not   find   it.
But it's nothing I thought about.
Eventually I realize I often can't find something—the
    Netflix envelope, the can opener cover, a letter, a
    garment.
These are not misplacements of an hour or two but rather
    days or always.
Not finding something is akin to the time I ran a course I
    had run for years never running out of breath.
Now I do not run *out* of breath, but there is less breath or
    more breath—whatever.
I won't stop running.
I won't run as often nor as far, but I
    will run as long as I can run.
And now I know that day when I cannot run may come...
    soon and not later.
I walk as much and as fast, but now I hear my breath,
    breath I never noticed but know was there.
The eyes join the failings.
I can't read the phone book but blame it on the phone
    company: font size was reduced to include zip codes,
    I know.
More and more the font size in newspapers, magazines,
    and books is not as small as much as it is blurred.
It can be read but read more easily with the $1.00 store
    glasses.

The doctor says the eyes are fine, but the owner of the
    eyes knows the eyes are not fine.
Eyes do not do what they used to do.
Experience tells me much in life is worse than instances
    cited here.
Granted.
No argument.
Yet the selfish me wants none of this for myself nor
    others.
The alternative to ageing is not my desire.
But I am not at the point of happily embracing ageing.

04/25/11

Georgia's Time

In Georgia's Time there would have been no wars
No slavery nor slave castles
No Trail of Tears
No Jim Crow Laws
No Wounded Knee
No Holocaust
No Bataan Death March
No Japanese internment
No lynchings
No apartheid
No bombings
No assassinations
No miseducation

NO HATE PERIOD.

And we would all be healthy and happy all of the time.
But there is no Georgia's Time, or little that counts.
And, as such there is/was all of the above in God's Time.
Surely God in His omniscience has a plan.
And this plan permitted/allowed/failed to stop
all of the above.
Perhaps one day, in the same way, long after
Georgia's Time, God's action and inaction
may be clear.
For now the only answer is simple: in God's
Time, only in God's Time.

05/13/10

Make the Call

Make the call.
You make the call.
Somebody has to make it.
There can be no change without a call.
Too often nobody wants to make the call.
So often everybody wants somebody else to
make the call.
Others are urged to make the call.
But anybody can't make the call.
You make the call.

06/03/10

To the Folks Who Didn't Want the Divorce*
(sane people, not those who believe they own their mates
and "If I can't have you, no one will.")

Nobody set out to hurt you.
You tried.
You did nothing or not very much wrong.
You may very well have done a lot right.
You most likely did what you believe is right.
You are not necessarily flawed.
You sacrificed.
You probably gave up some hopes and wishes
and dreams.
This is known, appreciated, considered, valued,
and evaluated information.
This was a decision made by the one who filed
or told you to file for the divorce, the one
who wants the divorce.

In a weird way, the one who wants the divorce
does not want the divorce.
Please don't laugh; don't be disgusted; don't
say, "What does 'is' mean?"
The one who wants the divorce probably did not set out to
hurt you.
This person also did nothing or not very much
wrong.
This person also did a lot right.
This person also did what was believed right.
This person also is not necessarily flawed.

This person also sacrificed.
This person also gave up some hopes and wishes
and dreams.
This person also tried, really tried, tried a long
time.
This person never said how hard trying was.
That trying, eventually, was not sufficient.
That trying reduced little or no pain.
That trying often caused pain—for both.
That trying ignored wants and needs, some of
which you did not know for myriad reasons.
This person had this need, a need not always
apparent, expressed, admitted, acknowledged.
You who want no divorce may have a need too!
The difference between us: This person acted
on the need.
The closer the end gets, the worse the idea of
staying is.
Stifling, choking, suffocating—all seem a reality
about to happen
Not because of you, not because of the one who
wants the divorce.
Space, space is the only answer.
The vow made in earnest to you, God, before anyone
present is broken, often broken very early but
not necessarily maliciously.
No one could have known what the couple had
or could become.

No one could have known, though some might
have guessed.
With two persons working, not knowing how
dissimilar their goals, this end is good,
definitely better than the lie this
would-be-divorced person lives and—by
association—you live.

05/15/10, 06/03/10

Evidence

Trembling fingers
Shaking hand
Fading memory
Weakening eyes
Aching knees
Collapsing legs
Burning feet
Wheezing breath:

All of the above can be obvious signs the body is
deteriorating, returning to the dust it was.
However, these are not the only signs.
And nothing says anyone will get any sign.
The day of the breaking down is often not the least bit
apparent, one more reason to do what we have to do
and want to do—mindful, of course, that hurting may
add to the harm.
There may be no time to look for evidence.

06/03/10

Tests

Tests.

All kinds of tests.

Self tests.

People tests.

God tests.

God asks us to put Him to the test.

We pass.

We fail.

We want to try again, sometimes.

We want to be retested, sometimes.

I want to move to the next course, with a clean slate in hopes of passing the next test.

10/08/10

Figs, Pomegranates, and Grapes

Delivered from the slavery of powerful Egypt
Ruled by a mighty Pharaoh whose might failed
to stop them.
Walked through wilderness full of who knows
what
Shod feet with shoes impenetrable
Clothed in permanent attire
Led by a pillar of cloud by day
Guided by a pillar of fire by night
Drank water from a rock
Ate manna from heaven
Crossed the Red Sea!

What a God they had!
My God!

And they and their short memories wanted to go
back to Egypt where they could eat figs,
pomegranates, and grapes!

6/3/10

06/03/10

What If?

What if Judas is in heaven?
Really.
Jesus told the thief on the cross: "Today shalt
thou be with Me in Paradise."
We know Judas was remorseful, so much so
that he hanged himself.
What if he was forgiven and is now in
heaven?
What if betraying Jesus was what Judas was supposed to do?

What if his assignment was to betray Jesus?
Jesus had to be killed, so said God: without shedding of blood is no remission of
sins.
What if Judas did not have the option of
saying, "I refuse this mission"?
What if the crowd had the assignment to yell,
"Crucify Him!"
What if the soldiers had the assignment to kill
Jesus?

What if all of us are given assignments—assignments we can't refuse, exchange, or
ignore?
What if some of us have heinous moves such
as Judas', the crowd's, the soldiers',
and others of us get to look on?

What if our assignments are to look at and
comment on the action?

Do we belittle Judas, or do we believe that he could be forgiven?
Do we point at him, claim we would never have done such a deed, or do we say,
"There but for the grace of God go I?"

What if God is looking at each of us,
considering our responses?
What if He is keeping track of the times we do
not feed the hungry, visit the sick or imprisoned?
What if God notes each time we did or did not turn the other cheek, walk that
second mile,
give up our coats and cloaks?

What if that Desiderata person is right and everything, everything is unfolding as it
should?
What if?

02/20/10

The Inconvenience of Being Intelligent

Dedicated to President Barak H. Obama

The smart person is so often at great peril.
There are inconveniences, disadvantages.

The quick-witted, thinking individual has unspoken rules.
Suck up names such as Brains, Brilliantine, Geek and Nerd.
Limit vocabulary and concepts, second nature.
Forego the allusions, analogies, and allegories.
Forget the anecdotes.
Explain the irony and parallels.
Reduce the similes and metaphors.
Avoid cutting the opposition to shreds—with words, of course.
Suffer fools—without ever seeming to do so.
Laugh with never at the stupid.
Prepare to explain and explain again.
List all the steps all the time.
Listen to issues irrelevant—at least at the time.
Hear and rehear tales well known or easily guessed.
Repeat shared history, mutual experiences.

Hide impatience of enumerating.
Conceal the frustration of narrating.
Smother spontaneity.
Regulate, if not eliminate, passion.
Play along with what they see as their superiority.
Learn confidence may be mistaken for arrogance.
Know not to know some answers or too many answers.
Make errors.
Feign ignorance.
Don't set curves too high.
These are some of the perils, the disadvantages of being smart.

02/20/10

Detour

I wonder what went through the minds of
Goodman, Schwerner, and Cheney once run off the road...
Did they think, I had no idea it would end like
this, I knew it would end like this, I
wish it had not ended like this?
I can imagine Cheney knowing what would happen—at least knowing the end: he
would die.
Goodman and Schwerner probably pointed out to the Klansmen something the
Klansmen
knew: the Klansmen were violating their rights, the Klansmen could not kidnap them.
The two young men had no idea such hatred existed although they were in Mississippi
because such hatred existed.
The two young men probably had no idea they would be killed.

They were in Mississippi because there were
folks who paid no attention to the rights of black folk or folks who wanted rights for
black
folks
And they did not think their rights would be taken, certainly not their lives.
In the midst of their teaching and helping, they were being taught and helped.

How afraid were they?

Most of us will never know such fear.
But they must have eventually come to understand what so many blacks understood
and had
understood for a very long time.

All of us owe Goodman, Schwerner, and Cheney.

The horror of what happened to them and its worldwide coverage opened some eyes and minds, convinced some that an America such as that required change, that an America such
as that should not be.

And yet, yet, the Southern Poverty Law Center can cite instances of such brutality prevalent
today.
Yes, despite the detours, many of us have yet to get on the right road.

April 2010

Galloping

All four hooves off the ground at the same time.
We know it happens.
Muybridge's camera shows it.
A horse galloping.
Peter Shaffer transferred galloping to people—living life to the fullest
Most folks don't know galloping exists.
Far fewer folks know galloping exists but won't gallop for fear of the risks.
An ever so small group of folk gallop.
.
I confess.
I grasp the metaphor.
I'm in that third group—most of the time.
I work to be in the third group most of the time.
I've left cave after cave because of my desire
to gallop.
What did Judy sing?
"If pretty little blue birds fly, then why oh
why can't I?"
If horses, far bigger than I, can gallop, then why can't I?

04/26/10

Jessica Madlock's painting *Storm Runner* was
drawn to accompany *Galloping*.

Makings

Culture
Two syllables
Multiple components
Setting
Heredity

Community

Religion
History
Education
The mix? The Mix! The mix.

11/29/10

Desperation

"Men lead lives of quiet desperation." Thoreau.
No! No, I said.
Of course, some men lead lives of quiet desperation.
But not *men, not all men* ...

That was then, in my youth.
But as companies outsource and downsize
As fewer jobs say "no experience necessary"
As jobs no longer come with pensions and "usual" benefits
As people get laid off a few years before collecting pensions
As people helplessly watch pension funds dissolve
As pensions fail to cover what was expected
As people look for jobs at age fifty and above
As adult children return home to live
As adult married children with children return home to live
As college graduates can't find employment
As house notes can't be made
As taxes can't be paid
As neighborhoods deteriorate
As property values deflate
As health insurance is inadequate
As home insurance warns us to watch the losses or inquiries about losses
As dreams of paying off a mortgage vanish
As the threat of losing belongings becomes reality...
OK, I see.
All of those men and women who don't have tons of dollars may indeed lead lives
of quiet
desperation.

12/29/10

Misreading

Someone does not show up.
The disappointed one thinks the reason is lack of care.
But the reason may be the wealth of care.
An expected yes comes out no.
But the reason may be the unfathomable cost of yes.

A gift does not arrive.
The would-be giver arrived but could not present self and gift.

In each instance words cannot provide a satisfactory answer.
Actions don't always solve problems.
Nobody planned the result.
And yet, someone, one whom we may love most, seems always to misread, to think we
Could've or should've or couldn't have done, stayed less or more, given more or less.

Many are the ones mangled from misreading.

11/24/10

The Other Brother: The Non-Prodigal Son

Always at Daddy's beck and call
Always prompt and willing
Never disrespectful
Never a complaint
Never taking advantage
No dreams of leaving
No rebelling
No requests
Just giving, giving, giving

And then one day his younger brother, better known as the prodigal, returns.

The younger brother was never at Daddy's beck and call
Never prompt and willing
Usually disrespectful
Regularly complaining
Always taking advantage
Began early dreaming of leaving
Always rebelling
Always requesting
Just taking, taking, taking

Daddy's response at the return: a huge party, great gifts of clothes and jewelry.

There's something to be said for following dreams and making requests.

But you decide what.

03/01/10

No Ram in the Bushes

Isaac—lucky, fortunate, blessed, some say.
Abraham kept his son though willingly placing him on the altar.
Bold Abraham
Faithful Abraham
Obedience is better than sacrifice.
Abraham obeyed.
Son Isaac saved
Ram sacrificed

O for a ram, more often, for more of us!

Those soldiers on both sides
Those murdered missionaries
Those civil rights workers
Those children who integrated schools
Those molested children
Those victims of drunk drivers
The battered everywhere

What did they do?
What didn't they do?
Where were their rams?
Why were there no rams?

Oh, for a ram, more often, for more of us.

This is a time for rams, many rams
Because daily we are sacrificed as we sacrifice.

Oh, for a ram, more often, for more of us.

Oh, for a ram.

Remember His saying, "My God, My God, why..."
Somebody said, "Where was the ram for Jesus?"

Could the answer be "There aren't enough rams, or rams don't like being sacrificed"?
Maybe rams protest.

02/25/10

No Compromise

"Regardless of the decision, don't leave,"
the woman pleaded.
Members on neither side doubted her sincerity.
Both sides wanted a whole.
What she did not know is opponents could not imagine
a whole with such disparate parts.
Such a whole could not materialize.
Go or stay.
Black or white.
Good or bad.
True or false.
There is no compromise.
Rarely is this true.
But sometimes it is.
Sometimes it is.

03/03/11

Ways

My way
Clear.
Certain.
Correct.
Confident.
Uncompromising.

A wish!

Singer Frank Sinatra and songwriter Paul Anka as well as the rest of us are fortunate
we get
to live parts of our lives our way.

Singer and songwriter had far more money than I, so more often perhaps they lived
their way, traveled more highways and
byways far more often than I.
But too much in life is a variable for me to believe either did it all his way.
Too much takes no notice of us for us to have our way all the day each day.
Yet I am grateful there are those choices we
make which make ways.
I have no doubt that some events in their
lives were the ways of somebody else or at
least a combination of ways, not quite
their ways.

02/2005

Michelangelo Unfinished

See, perhaps the man Michelangelo wasn't so
> different from the rest of us—in preparation and inspiration.

Unfinished are some of his pieces, some say.
As finished as Michelangelo wanted them to be,
> others say.

What about as finished as he was, as we are?
Why can't some of the sculptures be a symbolic replica of
> what we human beings are?

Aren't we always becoming?

All of our frailties and failures
Our unmet needs
Our squashed desires and destroyed dreams
Our settling
Our limited space and more limited time—
Our incompleteness is completed by all of the secrets we dare
> not share.

Regularly and randomly we stop or are stopped in the midst
> of a process.

Who's to say emerging does not depict most accurately?

04/27/09, 01/24/12

Journeys

You can take a bus, train, or plane.
You can ride a horse, camel, or elephant.
You can run or jog.
You can walk rain or shine.
I have done all of the above.

But some of my most memorable journeys have been those
    in the mind, those in which the physical distance was zero inches but
    the mental and/or spiritual distance immeasurable.
Loved ones won't always be around, despite
    what they say or I believe.
Folks nor I do not and sometimes cannot always see what
    we wish each other to see.
Love does not solve all problems.
We cannot and do not always keep our word.
We will let down and be let down.
We cannot always escape ourselves regardless of the places
    we go.
But having made the mental journeys, all the physical
    journeys are better and more meaningful.

Bon Voyage!

05/25/11

The Right Thing

"I'm so tired of doing the right thing!"
She had thought this more than once.
Now she screamed it.

Attending meetings she did not want to attend
Worshipping when she did not feel like worshipping
Writing letters she did not want to write
Visiting folks whom she did not wish to visit
Paying bills she did not make nor want to pay
Being polite when she did not want to be polite
Answering questions she did not want to answer
Making loans she did not need nor want to make
Giving gifts she did not want to give...

And then a question was posed: "Who says what is right?"

"Maybe," said the speaker, "If you do not want to do,
    maybe what you're doing is not the right thing to
    do."
And she answered, "Responsibility may not be all it's cracked
    up to be, but it is necessary, especially in a
    civilization."

03/01/10

The Impossible Win

Censure, disapproval, exclusion, rejection,
Hate repeatedly heaped!

Why should we be surprised when
        someone gives up, runs away, bails out?
The well-prepared do not always escape.
Only the strong and extremely lucky survive.
And so many of us keep asking folks to get
        stronger.
We command, "Take that."

The person does—and on both sides is
        surprise.

        Openly and secretly we say, "Well, I bet you can't take this?"
        And the person does.
Stunned, we grab more damaging ammunition.

No equality here!
Some folks just can't take this.

05/12/09

The Straw Speaks

The straw got a bad rap, a bum deal if you
        will.
Before the straw was placed on the camel's
        back, a mattress was there.
So were two wicker chairs and a table.

The weight.
Oh, the weight!
The cud-chewing beast of burden was true to
        his role.

But there's a limit!
The straw is hereby exonerated.
The straw did not break the camel's back.
The straw happened to be in the wrong place
        at the right time.

And there are those who understand the straw's view.

04/03/06

Visitors

Cedar Creek, Clallam Bay, Coyote Ridge, McNeil Island, Mission Creek,
Monroe, Stafford Creek, Washington State
Add Walla Walla.

For the uninitiated, the above are Washington State prisons.
Not everyone knows these names.
More men than women live in these places.
But more women than men visit these
        places.
Mothers, grandmothers, sisters, aunts,
        daughters, girlfriends, the rare dad, brother, or
        uncle, all ages
They arrive early.
Truly good friends don't get out of the
        vehicles—amazing friends.
They come along to keep their visitor
        friends company, to stay with the
        children, to help with the children.
Visitors usually have a scrubbed-down
        look, some dressed in what was called
        Sunday best.
A few may wear something too tight or too short, too low.
Obligatory, guilty, angry, sad, they come.
Always specified days and times—who
        cares how far visitors must travel or
        if jalopies can make the trip?
Put belongings in locker.
Empty pockets.

Remove jewelry.
Shoes or bras can set off metal detectors.
Wait outside until the keepers let you in.
Wait your turn.
Wait some more.
Purchase a card to purchase refreshments.
Purchase too much; spend it the next visit.
Purchase too little; go back to where you
    began to purchase again.
The logic of who is called when rests with the
    authorities.
How long it takes the called to arrive—
    another mystery.
If men only knew what visitors
    endure to visit, maybe they wouldn't
    break the law and never a second time!

April 2005

Hair Hazards

Generations of women endured and endure
    Hot combs
    Strong chemicals
    Burned scalps
    Scarred necks
And other unknown, unspeakable, possibly worse injuries
All for the sake of beauty
All in the name of beauty.

As we contributed and contribute to the coffers of
    billionaires who routinely failed/fail to see the beauty
    we ourselves often do not routinely see.

05/11/11

Elephant in the Room

Mom sews.
Dad reads.
It's not that there isn't anything else to do.
It isn't that both would not rather be doing something else.
He does what he believes is outwardly expected.
She does what she believes is outwardly expected.
Many outsiders observing say, "Oh, what a lovely couple."
The couple smile politely.
But Dad knows just about anywhere else is better than here.
Ditto for mom.
What neither knows is for once, the first time in a long time, they are on the same page: one is as unhappy as the other!
BUT everything they have ever been taught says do what's outwardly expected.
So, she sews and he reads while an elephant has taken up residence in their midst.
Neither acknowledges the elephant.
Too bad the elephant does not talk.

Inspired by Jessica Dodge's painting *Daily Mirror 2005*   *10/14/05*

My Poems

A revelation: my poems are always about me—
> my feelings, my perspectives, my conclusions, my
> aspirations, my inclinations, my faults, my flaws, my
> triumphs.

My poems are always my view, at a mirror or through a
> prism, clear or distorted—knowingly or not—up close or
> at a distance.

My poems are the product of my imagination, my
> observation.

I am the subject of my poems, with varying prominence.
I am the subject, not always the first person, sometimes
> third, but the best objective observer I can be at the
> time.

I am the narrator
I write.
I rule.
Ridiculed sometimes,
Misunderstood sometimes,
Liked sometimes,
Appreciated sometimes,
Loved sometimes,
Dismissed sometimes.
Awakened sometimes.
Whatever...
Constrained by all that is me, I write.
When I write, I rule—if only as I write.

03/15/11   Inspired by Adam Korpak's illustration *Rocket Writer Rules*

Why I Won't Let It Go

Why won't I let it go, you ask.

Do you honestly think I prefer not letting go?

Letting go is not as simple as you seem to think.
If it were, I would.

You believe I prefer the cooling or eliminating of
 friendships, the cost?

I do not.
I would prefer not to have a battle raging.

I have let go much, still do.
But everything cannot be let go.
Doesn't everybody have some things that can't be let
 go or can't be let go unless they are resolved?
Doesn't everyone have a core that defies crumbling?

Peace is one of the few causes I won't let go.
I want peace; I want peace all of the time.
I'll fight for it.
But always acquiescing to the other's point of view to
 end the hostility is not peace.
Peace is much more than cessation of fighting
 or hostility.
Much means little or nothing to me.
Less means more, but I can compromise.

A few principles, however, have no space for
    compromise.
Getting to them, accepting them, abiding by them has
    not always been easy, but I have managed.
I call these principles my core.
This core is not easily changed.
Something traumatic must happen before my core
    changes.
I know.
I have tried letting go only to be frustrated with
    myself, others, and/or God.
I've learned: no trauma, no significant change.
So, when I won't let something go, believe me, the
    something has traveled through many filters.
Until the problem is gone, I won't let go.

03/09, 10/11

Passing Moments

Most moments simply pass.
Some moments we want to cradle.
Some moments we want to erase.
Some moments define us.
Those moments can make or break us.
We can describe a success or failure with equanimity.
But the effects, oh the effects.
Ages hence we can cite the circumstance
      Because a moment did not simply pass.

11/27/10

Crazy Men

First the daddy called her Lips or Legs, a name over which she had no control,
about as much
control as she had over Dad's name-calling.
Then the classmate wanted to know why her hair was so short, said all of his
sisters had long hair.
The husband wanted to know why she cut her hair so short—looked like a
man, he said.
He criticized the color, telling her she had passed the age for that color.
Later others said she had shoulders like a man.
One man once chimed in about what he called her big feet.
These crazy boys and men can do great damage to girls and women who may
be only less crazy than they.
Too often the impressions linger, but may eventually disappear.
Most likely, however, another group, sane by any standard,
May be marked for a long time, maybe a lifetime.
The crazy men—especially the ones important in the lives of
the girls—too often leave indelible scars, scars visible to the females alone.
The speakers go about their business.
The hearers, however, may be stymied by
the unasked-for assessments and allow them to interfere with their journeys.

06/14/11

Observing the Creative Process

I have to be more disciplined.
I am writing a poem and listening to the television.
Somebody says a word I do not recognize.
I stop to look it up—"No results found," says WORD's
    dictionary.
Back to the poem I go—but, then I check dictionary.com.
Yes, "No results found."
Return to the poem.
Answer the phone.
Kitchen timer calls.
The doorbell rings.
Check weather in Indiana.
Remove clothes from washer.
Return to poem.
Get that greeting card in the mailbox.
Eat cereal.
Answer the vibrating cell.
A land call interrupts.
Mail carrier rings the doorbell.
Return to poem.
Focus.
Focus on the finish.
Reread the whole.
Cancel thoughts of sick friend.
Get ready for the dentist.
Think about the poem.
Make the dermatologist appointment.
Head for the door.

Wait!
Write one more line.
There it is! There it is!
I can do this.
I have done this again.
Another creation is born.
Tomorrow the work file may claim the poem.
But for now, the poem is done.

06/14/11 Inspired by Adam Korpak's illustration *Writing Takes Form*

The Way Some of Us Are

Carver's knife found shut, said *The Seattle Times*.
No exclamation necessary.
A period is all there is.
No one knows how not surprised
        many folks are.
A human being shot, killed another human
        being.
That's the truth, the fact.
That one human being is white and the other a
        Native American is a fact and often a
        problem.
The former is a policeman; the latter a carver.
Too often that is a problem.
I submit that if both had looked at each other as
        human beings there would've been no
        killing.
I submit that the white policeman saw red long
        before he saw human being.
I submit that many policemen often see a color
        before they see a person.
I submit much of the policeman's culture says
        beware of people of color, the darker they,
        the more careful you.
I submit the policeman believed he was in
        danger though he with his gun was
        not close enough to see a closed knife.

And I submit, diminished mental state
	notwithstanding, Mr. Williams knew much
	of this and chose to risk being himself.

No doubt there is sorrow; there should be.
But absolutely no amount of sorrow nor
	anything else, nothing will bring back Mr.
	John T. Williams.
Of course, policemen do not want to be killed.
Of course, they must protect themselves.
But as long as they serve a populace they fear,
	we can count on too many of them
	stomping, beating, and shooting, killing
	too—acting and then asking questions.
The cold-blooded killings of their comrades
	doubtlessly makes them more guarded.
Until policemen know more of the folks they are
	guarding we can expect them to feel justified
	in their actions despite being deadly wrong.

11/10/11

Created to Do God's Work

(to Pacific Northwest American Baptist Women)

Jeremiah 29:11 For I know the plans I have for you," declares the LORD, "plans to prosper you and not to harm you, plans to give you hope and a future." -NIV

I don't think God asks us to climb Mt. Everest or
    even Mt. Rainier.
I don't believe He expects us to circumnavigate the
    world in an open boat.

But I do believe God wants us to love and serve
    and worship Him.
I believe we worship Him when we
    love and minister to as many of His children
    as we can—and we are
    His children created to do His work.

We can minister by doing any of the following:

Flashing a smile
Saying please
Responding thank you
Giving a nod
Opening, holding, closing a door
Making a bed
Picking up litter
Wiping away a tear
Cleaning hand, foot, or backside

Holding or caressing a hand
Nurturing a child
Planting a flower
Cleaning a house
Extending a hand
Lending an ear
Preparing a dish or a meal
Entertaining a guest
Accompanying a friend or stranger
Running an errand
Teaching a class
Checking some figures
Delivering a message
Encouraging the discouraged
Supporting the weak
Explaining the problem
Offering a solution
Writing a letter
Heeding a call
Contributing to a cause
Waiting to help
Visiting the sick
Sending an e-mail
Fulfilling a request
Singing a song
Mending a quarrel
Playing a tune

Preparing to serve
Reading to the ill or blind
Mailing a card
Supporting what's right
Condemning what's wrong

Showing, telling, doing, acting, relating—
All plus more CAN be God's work for those we
        know and love and those we don't know!
What are we doing?
Why are we doing it?
Glorifying God in our every move—that is our
        destiny.
Glorifying God in our every move—that's our aim.
Glorifying God in our every move—that's what we are created for.

03/10

Slip-Sliding Syndrome

Sometimes we do not act because we don't care.
Other times we do not act because we care so much.
It's the slip-sliding syndrome.
We want to act.
We feel the need to act.
Yet we know the risk of acting wrongly, improperly.
We know we aren't afraid.
We want to improve and remedy.
But we know we may worsen and destroy.
Life has taught us, teaches us how easily our acts can be
>   misunderstood.
We know silence itself is an act.
Little judges and big judges surround us with their varying
>   fairness.
So we sit or stand immobilized…
>   all the time knowing someone may see us as uncaring,
>   disinterested, unresponsive, irresponsible.

But often we are none of the above.
Our concerns paralyze us.
There's no obvious movement.

But brainwaves and heartbeats are in a stage of frenzy.
We may even beat our breasts and chests rhythmically.
Logic and love are at their highest.
Perhaps the day will come when the beloved will see.

09/18/04

Hugs and Words

Some days I need hugs.
But most days I need more words than hugs.
Don't get me wrong.
Both can be great at the right time.
But any hug or word from anybody at any time won't do.
I love whole-hearted hugs.
I love worthwhile words.

The words and hugs I need have to be genuine.
And I cannot always tell this is so.
What I know is I'm tired of hollow hugs and worthless
        words.
Sometimes I instantly feel the hollowness and hear the
        worthlessness.
Other times I'm misled, dangerously deceived.
Or I recognize the deceit and remain polite.
And partake of the hypocrisy.

What am I to do?
Suppose something I see as hollow and worthless is neither.
Suppose the sincerity and honesty are true.
Hugs and words, two more items that may cause as many
        problems as present solutions.

06/13/11

Under the Big Top I

Step right up!
Join the fun.
Pop the whip.
You're as much a part of the show as the performers are.
If there's no audience, there's no show.
Come into the arena.
Join in.
The time here is limited.
Listen to the music.
See the real that's unnatural, like a fish out of water.
See the bodies contorted, distorted, upside down.
Note bodies "standing" not on two legs but two arms.
Observe bodies going in circles, always in circles,
> clowns dressed down making noise rather than music with their musical instruments,
> pigs dressed up pushing baby carriages rather than rooting in the dirt or wallowing in the mud,
> hats that connote authority worn by folk with no authority,
> aerialists walking on tightropes high above the ground.

The donkey sitting as donkeys do may be the only natural presence.

But this is the Big Top.
Be filled with awe!
Be dazzled!
Let theatrics overwhelm!

Keep looking, but don't look too closely.
Keep listening, but don't listen too closely.
Presiding are the not-hearing-evil first monkey, the not-seeing-evil second monkey, and the not-speaking-evil third monkey.
Presiding is the audience, the only irreplaceable member in the Big Top.
Remember, no audience, no show.
Like the monkeys, the audience members hear, see, and speak no evil—at times.
But permission is granted to do all three at the Big Top, a temporary escape from what may be a real-life house of flames.
Long live the Big Top.

Inspired by Jessica Dodge's painting *Under The Big Top 2005*   *10/14/05*

Under the Big Top II

People pay to see

>Dogs and elephants standing on two legs
>Horses jumping through hoops or going down ladders
>Geese dropping golden eggs

>Mice and elephants dressed in doilies

>All of these happenings.

Forget our knowing these happenings are not normal—
>whatever that is.

People are not under the Big Top to know; people don't want
>to know.

People want a break from knowing.
So people pay for all of these happenings.
A sucker is born every minute.
(Actually, the grand increase in the birth rate calls for an
>adjustment in the number.)

People continue to pour into the circus.
Forget the pay.
And one ring is not enough.
Americans, especially, need three rings, no one ring for us.
Maybe it's the red, white, and blue.
Hearing, seeing, and speaking the truth can really be a task.

So we scan here and peek there, never gazing in any one
>   place long.
After all, sitting under the Big Top requires less energy, is
>   less painful, and costs much less than sitting in the glass
>   house called Home.

Inspired by Jessica Dodge's painting *Under The Big Top 2005*   10/14/05

A Dozen Commandments to Know

Thou shalt know the same word may have different
    meanings.
Thou shalt know some persons never learn what we want
    them to learn and we never learn what they want us tolearn!
Thou shalt know some persons never value what we
    value.
Thou shalt know all who know better do not do better.
Thou shalt know fair is rare.
Thou shalt know everyone does not care about us.
Thou shalt know chances of being hurt are tremendous
    regardless of our actions or sincerity.
Thou shalt know we are the sum of what happened to us
    AND what did not happen to us.
Thou shalt know people, favorites included, do not always
    tell the truth.
Thou shalt know telling the truth does not always set us
    free solve, or end a problem.
Thou shalt know people—intentionally and
    unintentionally, those who love us and those who hate us—can damage
    us, sometimes irreparably.
Thou shalt know that sometimes no one can love us as we
    want and need to be loved.

03/28/11

When Did It Begin?

When did it begin?
We'll never know.
Maybe it was the war—no, the conflict.
We know the military took its toll:
    banged knee, blood pressure, Agent Orange.
We know the time there was his longest two years ever.

When did it begin?
We'll never know.
Maybe it was at work—a job he'd held for years,
    doing a job that garnered him awards.
Then he made so many errors:
    little errors, big errors, expensive errors.
We know, "Sorry," they said, "but you must leave."

But when did it begin?
We'll never know.
Maybe it was the day he left the water running.
But it could have been when this chef omitted ingredients
    in a recipe.
Perhaps it was those times he the bill payer did not pay
    bills.
Oh, and there were all of those telemarketing orders he
    made.
We know he was no longer the efficient one we had known.

Now when did it begin?
We'll never know.

We know the first doctor said "dementia."
"Mild cognitive impairment," said another.
We've come to know when it began means nothing.
Knowing when is not always of any help.
The something in his head has no meaning for listeners.
He uses recognizable words but with absolutely no order.
Anyone who has heard says, "I can't explain it" or "I
      can't imitate it."
What we do know is that we do not want to come to this
      end.

01/23/12

Warfare

I've said it before.
I'll say it again.
We cannot have war and fair.
The two are mutually exclusive.
All is fair in war.
Regardless of treaties and conventions,
ALL IS FAIR IN WAR.
Collateral damage in the form of children, women, and men; pink mist from any of these or
the armed, designated enemy; death count or not from the "good" and "bad,"
Calleys and Wuterichs will always be present.
Many names we'll never know; they get to keep their stories and lies and truths to themselves—or release them in the form of violence on family, friends, persons unknown, the society.
Some will be tried; others won't.
Some will be imprisoned; others won't.
And maybe they will have no peace.
But they will not be alone, sometimes with us, other times with ghosts of the enemy.
And all of us will pay, in varying ways and varying amounts, true, but all of us will pay.

United States Army Lieutenant William Laws Calley, Jr. was found guilty of murdering twenty-two unarmed South Vietnamese civilians in the My Lai Massacre March 16, 1968, during the Vietnam War.
United States Marine Frank Wuterich and his men killed twenty-four Iraqi civilians November 19, 2005, after a Marine died in an insurgent attack. Eventually Wuterich was honorably discharged.

01/25, 26/12

Vocabulary Building

Conflicts and wars are enlarging my vocabulary.
Sometimes the name people take words that have a
    meaning for me and give those words a new meaning—*patriot,* for example.
The name people love words related to Native Americans:
    Blackhawk, Tomahawk, Geronimo...
But there are other words, phrases and acronyms:
    Weapons of Mass Destruction or WMD
        Pink Mist
Friendly Fire   Collateral Damage
    Escalate Surge   PTSD
    Actionable Intelligence   I. E. D.

I must remember "strategic withdrawal" is more than
    withdrawal—or less than?
"Enhanced interrogation" is torture, something the
    USA does not do.
"Renditioned" means kidnapped.

All of the following are synonyms for "kill": liquidate
    with extreme prejudice, surgical strike, engage,
    contact...
Whatever happened to words such as *Creation, Order,*
    Decency, Humanity, Friend?
We are surrounded by so many weapons of mass
    distraction.
And make no mistake: too many of us are distracted.
Meanwhile, my vocabulary keeps growing as I long for
    the use and application of some of the old words and
    their old meanings.

10/03 Revised 02/12   Inspired by Selma Waldman's drawing *Skelani Soldier*

The Fray

You often get to choose where to stand in a fray:

Above

                                      Center

Beneath

To the left

                                                                                   To the right.

But know that in some frays anywhere but IN the fray is
    a less dangerous place to be.

01/17/12

Relationships

What he/she said and heard
and
what she/he said and heard
are quite different although they were the two parties of the same conversation.
He/She said he/she knew her/him.
She/He said he/she didn't know her/him, he/she only thought he/she knew her/him.

Then one day it occurred to her/him that he/she might indeed know her/him very well.

06/06/06

The Change

He changed lanes.
She answered the cell.
He texted.
He dived off the pier.
He pulled the trigger in the game.
He swerved in the dune buggy.

Each committed an act done many times.
But this time, something changed.
This time, something went wrong.
And all of them must adapt to the change.
And others must adapt too.
We can blame the actors.
They sometimes blame themselves.
Most sometimes say, "What if?"
No answer satisfies.
Never has, never will.

But what about receivers of the actions?
What about mourners and caregivers?
No answer satisfies.
Never has, never will.

08/26/11

Dead Soldiers

Dead.
Soldiers are dead.
Enemy fire, friendly fire—
Does it matter?
The soldiers are dead.
An IED, a mine, a bomb—
All kill.
The soldiers are dead.
A helicopter shot down
A cargo plane down
The soldiers are dead.
First deployment, fifth deployment
A homicide, a suicide
The soldiers are dead.
Tour after tour after tour
The end of a marriage
Separation from children
Withdrawal from friends
A different kind of death
At least a chance for a partial recovery
But too often the soldiers are dead.
Dead.

08/25/11

Two Women Talk About Death, Briefly

Of the death the great aunt said,
"I'm grateful God gave him to us twenty-two years. He
      did what God wanted him to do."
The friend said "I'm glad you have that attitude.
      That's so good."

What the friend thought was "I wish I could
      say that. I wish I could mean that."

What the aunt said may indeed be true, but the friend couldn't say it, never
      had and probably never would.

02/14/12

Demands

The pastor clearly said to the little girl and everyone else
    at the Sunday worship service: "You can make demands on God."
Years later the young woman understood that God, like
    many of the everyday people she knew, does not
    always execute our demands.

2000

Thirty Time

At **sixteen** he knew what he'd never do, knew what he'd
 always do, knew his goals, knew those goals would
 become reality.
He knew everything his small mind could fathom, routinely ignored his
 dumb parents.
Never giving, always getting, he was invincible, he
 thought.

At **twenty-one** he knew a little less than everything, had
 reduced his goals insignificantly, retained the
 invincibility.
Did speak to his parents, but only about himself, his
 successes, reminded them how they had failed.
Put all faith in himself and told everyone of his
 superiority.

At **thirty**, however, he readily admitted he knew very
 little.
Knew never to say "never" nor "always."
Knew he could make no guarantees.
"Maybe" became part of his vocabulary, so did "I don't
 know."
Had himself fallen and witnessed too many falls, knew
 doorstops do stop, and, worse, floods, earthquakes,
 tornadoes, and hurricanes do come but not on a
 schedule.
Too many variables ignore his wants, needs, presence.

What's more, his used-to-be dumb parents now know a
>lot.
His scarred golden hands, attesting his talent and skill, are
>open to give and get.
Vulnerability taking hold, he acknowledges an Alpha and
>Omega, sees the logic imbedded in yin and yang.

Somewhere after thirty he learned the certainties are
>water, air, earth, and fire, and their certainty is their
>existence, not their state or position.
More aware of his vulnerability, he momentarily
>wondered about all the years he hoped to have ahead
>of him and what he could possibly learn.
But by now he knew enough to know he could not
>possibly know what one might know by the time of
>seventy.

11/04 Inspired by Scott Mansfield's sculpture *The Time of Thirty*

Characters

I miss Willy Loman and Linda, Walter Lee and Mama,
        Oedipus, Hamlet, The Hunger Artist, Lear, and Mrs.
        Hutchinson and even Old Man Warner.

More and more I think of Hemingway's waiters in that
        clean, well-lighted place and how I am more
        like the older one than I could ever have imagined.

I still smile at the Old Man at the Bridge, the one
        who thought saying he was "without politics"
        would remove him from the fog and clarity" of
        war.

For more than a quarter century I welcomed a
        rendezvous several times a year with
        these real characters.

They came to be my friends because of what I
        learned from them, sometimes what to do but
        almost as often what not to do.

They refreshed my memory, always energized and
        motivated me, engaged me.

Of course I passed this information to folks who
        willingly and unwillingly accepted it.

I tried and hoped, probably prayed they would get,
        be inspired by the information.

I wanted them to have legitimate, safe shortcuts.

Decades later, occasionally sooner, I hear from
        characters who see what I saw or sometimes
        more than I saw.

And I miss the real characters more.
I relish having met them and regret so many meet
        them so late or, worse, never.
Oh, I can visit them whenever I choose, go straight
        to lines, often quote the lines, but nothing
        matches my meetings with them and a group
        of folks who willingly and unwillingly meet
        the real characters.

Teaching may not be the oldest, is definitely not
        the most lucrative profession, but it is by far the
        most rewarding endeavor I have ever undertaken.

05/13/11

INDEX

Age	91
All Ifs and Thens	1
An Attempt at Humor	21
Art Interrupts	74
Attention	88
Being Slow	36
Beliefs	56
A Bio	14
Brainprint	54
The Change	150
Chaos	42
Characters	156
Choices	40
Crazy Men	129
Created to Do God's Work	133
Dead Soldiers	151
Demands	153
Dependent Clauses	81
Desperation	109
Detour	105
A Dozen Commandments to Know	143
Elephant in the Room	124

Escapists	15
Evidence	98
Excuses	29
Familiarity	31
Few Corrections	39
Figs, Pomegranates, and Grapes	100
Flags	38
The Fray	148
Freedom—Or the Lack Thereof	3
Frogs and Princes	82
From Like to Dislike	19
Galloping	107
Georgia's Law	65
Georgia's Time	93
Hair Hazards	123
The Hand and Time	24
The Help	29
How Much?	5
Hugs and Words	138
I Ask Why	51
If You Lived Here	87
The Impossible Win	119

The Inconvenience of Being Intelligent	103
Innocent Eggs	62
It's a Wrap	50
I Wish	63
Journeys	117
Letting Someone In	34
The Lie Continues	71
Lies	70
Limits	30
The Little Nothing Dress	85
Maggots	61
Make the Call	94
Makings	108
Mama Nadi Confesses	77
Matt	67
Memory, What We Remember	6
Michael	89
Michelangelo Unfinished	116
Mind and Matter	32
Misreading	110
Molehills Becoming Mountains	53
Moving On	66

Musings	27
My Head Tapes	44
My Poems	125
The Nastiest Word	59
No Boots on the Ground	20
No Compromise	114
No Ram in the Bushes	112
Not Always Possible	43
Not Enough Time	37
Obscenity	10
Observation	35
Observing the Creative Process	130
Obstacles	13
Opportunities	69
The Other Brother: The Non-Prodigal Son	111
The Paradox of Handling	49
Passing Moments	128
A Patch of Ground	52
The Photographer Artist	40
The Problem with Memories	83
Promise Kept	78
The Quick and the Dead	30
Real Mistake	81

Reassessment	7
Relationships	149
Relieving Pressure	2
Religion and Guns	73
The Right Thing	118
Routine	80
Selected Stories	76
Sleep	90
Slip-Sliding Syndrome	137
Soaring	79
Special Song	57
A Standstill	8
The Straw Speaks	120
The Subjectivity of Objectivity	48
Suggestions	4
Terror Colors	64
Tests	99
There Is No Half-Time	16
Things To Do	45
Thirty Time	154
To the Folks Who Didn't Want the Divorce*	95
Twins Born at Different Times	12
Two Women Talk About Death, Briefly	152

Under the Big Top I	139
Under the Big Top II	141
Visitors	121
Vocabulary Building	147
Vows Broken	25
Warfare	146
The Way Some Of Us Are	132
Ways	115
What If?	101
What She Has Become	17
When Did It Begin?	144
Windmills—Or Not	33
Why?	46
Why I Won't Let It Go	126
Words	32

About the Author

GEORGIA STEWART MCDADE, a Louisiana native who has lived in Seattle more than half her life, has enjoyed reading and writing as far back as she can remember. As a youngster she wrote and produced plays for her siblings and neighbors and collaborated with church youth to write plays for special occasions. After earning a Bachelor of Arts from Southern University, Master of Arts from Atlanta University, and Doctorate of Philosophy from University of Washington, the English major spent more than thirty years teaching at Tacoma Community College as well as a number of other institutions on all levels. As a charter member of the African-American Writers' Alliance (AAWA), McDade began reading her stories in public in 1991. She credits AAWA with making her regularly write poetry. For decades she has written poems inspired by art at such sites as Gallery 110, Seattle Art Museum, and Columbia City Gallery. She did editorials for Pacific Newspapers, especially the *South District Journal,* for four years. She volunteers as a reporter at community radio station KBCS (91.3 FM). Convinced all of us can learn to write well, McDade conducts a variety of writing workshops for all ages. "Good writing can force us to think and think critically; we can theorize, organize, analyze, and synthesize better," says she. A prolific writer, she has works in AAWA anthologies *I Wonder as I Wander, Gifted Voices, Words? Words! Words,* and *Threads.* Her works include *Travel Tips for Dream Trips,* questions and answers about her six-month, solo trip around the world; *Outside the Cave,* a collection of poetry; and numerous essays, stories, and poems. Among her several writing projects are the biography of her high school principal and journals kept during her travels.

www.ingramcontent.com/pod-product-compliance
Lightning Source LLC
Chambersburg PA
CBHW051947290426
44110CB00015B/2138